Beneficial Property Taxation for Emerging Market Countries

Ehtisham Ahmad • Giorgio Brosio

Beneficial Property Taxation for Emerging Market Countries

Addressing Climate Change and Post-Pandemic Recovery

palgrave
macmillan

Ehtisham Ahmad
Former IMF, Grantham Research Institute
London School of Economics and Political Science
London, UK

Giorgio Brosio
Campus Luigi Einaudi
University of Torino
Torino, Italy

ISBN 978-3-031-08611-3 ISBN 978-3-031-08612-0 (eBook)
https://doi.org/10.1007/978-3-031-08612-0

This Palgrave Macmillan imprint is published by the registered company Springer Nature Switzerland AG.
The registered company address is: Gewerbestrasse 11, 6330 Cham, Switzerland

Preface

The importance of an effective property tax has become clearer in the context of ensuring and financing a resilient provision of health care and basic services during the pandemic. The sustainable financing of basic services and facilitating access to private finance is also coming into focus in view of the investments needed for decarbonization and sustainable employment generation. Yet, the standard ownership-valuation model has been found wanting in advanced and emerging market countries alike. In this volume, we address issues that have arisen in practice since the 1980s, and some of the analytical and political economy considerations that have become apparent over the years in implementing alternative models. Rent-seeking due to the proximity of taxpayers and tax collectors has been a persistent problem, while resistance from taxpayers has increased over time. Both simplification of the tax base—for example, through area/location-based or presumptive tax, and use of functional administration structures provide important alternatives, supported by modern technological advances, for example, satellite imagery and blockchain options, together with low-tech verification.

We draw on a series of IMF technical assistance missions that we participated in on multilevel finance in emerging market countries in the mid-1990s (including Colombia, Indonesia, Bolivia, Nigeria, and Mexico). There were widespread and persistent difficulties in the design of a property tax to generate revenues with the "ownership-valuation property tax model" that applies in the US and many advanced economies, and which has been the standard recommendation of the multilateral banks to many countries. The complexity of establishing property titles or accurate and timely valuation changes had proved to be a major constraint. This was compounded in many cases by the proximity of tax administrators to taxpayers (e.g., the colonial "tax collector" model in some countries) generating "rent-seeking" opportunities.

We participated in an IMF technical assistance mission to Colombia in 1995 to address sub-national tax options and transfer design to support a significant decentralization of spending responsibilities that had just been initiated (Ahmad et al., 1995). Although Colombia had probably the best cadastral system in Latin America, revenue collections were dismal. The mission proposed the use of presumptive methods to break the logjam on property taxes, the introduction of a modern functional structure of local tax administration that would minimize rent-seeking, and an equalization transfer system to ensure that the tax system does not give an unfair advantage to the large metropolitan areas and exacerbate spatial imbalances. Given his dissatisfaction with the cadaster at that time, Mayor Mokus in Bogotá built on the functional administration and introduced a self-evaluation system together with a sanction of forced purchase of properties at declared values in egregious cases. After an initial spurt in revenues, collections stalled and remain below potential. It has not been easy also to replicate this in other cities in Colombia.

The political economy problem of placing additional taxes on fixed-income people makes, paraphrasing Alfred Marshall, the ownership-valuation model "onerous," and for most informal sector households inapplicable. Experiments with the model in Shanghai and Chongqing failed to raise significant revenues, and this has posed a significant constraint in anchoring the financing of local infrastructure that has relied heavily on land sales and off-budget accounts of property developers and urban development corporations. A major political economy constraint arises as in the Mexican case—the lack of accountability when rates are set at higher levels, but administration remains local.

Our proposals on area and location-based property taxes build on work in the 1980s in South Asia on presumptive methods of taxing agricultural land (Ahmad and Stern 1991), as well as the reforms in the UK in the early 1990s and in the transition economies in Eastern Europe. This considerably simplifies administration, that can be further streamlined with the use of satellite imagery and low-tech verification. And blockchain has huge potential, together with the use of big data and cross-referencing information from different sources. This was also a critical component of Mayor Mockus' agenda in Bogotá in the mid-1990s, a precursor to the use of big data but digital technological advances were not available at that time.

Despite the simplifications with occupancy rather than ownership, the area/locality-based taxes that are allowed to vary by band at the discretion of local authorities, and the high-tech identification of properties and tighter monitoring of transactions, the political economy constraints cannot fully be addressed without reference to the set of benefits provided by the local governments. This is essential to convert the "onerous" to a "beneficial" property tax. We made a thorough exploration of the tax-expenditure link in property taxation in Mexico in a chapter co-authored with Caroline Pöschl in our Handbook of Multilevel Finance (Ahmad and Brosio, 2015). We explored options to facilitate this transformation for Senegal and Tanzania (Ahmad, Brosio, and Gerbrandy, 2018) in a report for the European Commission (EC). Summaries of the two cases are included in this volume.

While there is excellent academic and policy-based work on cities, including metropolitan areas like Mexico City or Guangzhou, the issues related to informality and slums, as well as pandemics and climate change cannot be fully addressed without considering interactions across cities and incentives for workers to move in search of better economic opportunities. This formed the basis for a program at the LSE on Financing Sustainable Transitions in China and Mexico, financed by the UK BEIS through the Coalition of Urban Transitions. The work in China was undertaken jointly with a few Chinese Universities and the Chinese Academy of Social Science, and the property tax simulations were conducted by Ahmad with Meili Niu, Liming Wang, and Meiyan Wang (and the China Chapter is based on Ahmad, Niu, Wang and Wang, 2021). The Mexican simulations were undertaken jointly with Hernan Viscarra (and the Mexico Chapter draws on Ahmad and Viscarra, 2020).

London, UK; Turin, Italy

Ehtisham Ahmad
Giorgio Brosio

References

Ahmad E, N Stern, (1991) The theory and practice of tax reform in developing countries. Cambridge University Press.

Ahmad, E. and H. Viscarra (2020), "Financing Clean, Compact and Connected Cities in Mexico: role of a "beneficial" property tax," LSE Program on Sustainable Transitions in China and Mexico.

Ahmad, E., G. Brosio, P. Spahn and C. Vehorn (1995) Colombia: Reforming Territorial Taxation and Transfers, IMF Fiscal Affairs Department, Washington DC.
Ahmad E, G Brosio and C Pöschl, (2015) Local property taxes and benefits in developing countries: overcoming political resistance? In: Ahmad E, and Brosio G (eds) Handbook of Multilevel Finance. Edward Elgar, Cheltenham.
Ahmad E, Brosio G and Gerbrandy J., (2018) Property taxation Economic features, revenue potential and administrative issues in a development context. EU, Brussels.
Ahmad, E., Meili Niu, Liming Wang, Meiyan Wang, 2021. "Designing Beneficial Property Taxation for Sustainable Development in China—evidence from six cities, including Guangzhou" LSE Program on Financing Sustainable Urban Transitions in China and Mexico.

Contents

List of Figures

List of Tables

Introduction: Growing Importance of Beneficial Property Taxation in a Post-pandemic World

Abstract A stable and secure base for local basic services and infrastructure has become central in the policy debate to effectively manage economic, trade and financial shocks that increasingly affect the vulnerable, especially but not exclusively in developing countries. The pandemic has added to the fiscal pressures on local governments, given the negative impact on basic service provision including health care and education, especially for the vulnerable and informal sector. Climate change is adding new pressures that require abatement and adaptation policies, many of which fall in the sphere of interest, or competence of local government, entailing local production of global public goods. A perfect storm is generated through the disruptions to the global value chains, including for food and energy, due to the aftermath of geo-political tensions and conflict, and this is felt most acutely by vulnerable households where local governments are unable to ensure access to basic services and nutrition.

Property taxes in most G7 countries form the bedrock of local financing of basic services and access to private financing for investments. Yet the dismal performance of the property tax, even in countries like India and Mexico, with decades of experience and implementation, is largely due to political economy constraints associated with adjusting valuations on fixed-income households, as well as the difficulties in establishing ownership. We argue in this volume that it is possible to reform property taxes rapidly to address the growing needs of sustainable transitions and increased resilience, by linking the tax to local public services, and to base the recurrent tax on non-business properties on occupancy rather than ownership. A simpler functional administration model can reduce rent-seeking, supplemented by high-tech satellite monitoring of size and location, together with an increasing use of blockchain technology.

Keywords: Taxation of property • Tax reform • Sustainable urban growth • Local accountability • Tax-benefits links

The pandemic has added to the fiscal pressures on local governments, given the negative impact on basic service provision including health care and education, especially for the vulnerable and informal sector. Climate change is adding new pressures that require abatement and adaptation policies, many of which fall in the sphere of interest, or competence of local government, entailing local production of global public goods.

Property taxes in most G7 countries form the bedrock of local financing of basic services and access to private financing for investments. Yet the dismal performance of the property tax, even in countries like India and Mexico, with decades of experience and implementation, is largely due to political economy constraints associated with adjusting valuations on fixed-income households, as well as the difficulties in establishing ownership. This raises questions about the design of the tax and whether there is scope to address lacunae relatively quickly, given the dual challenges of recovery from the pandemic and addressing increasing risks from climate change.

We argue in this volume that it is possible to reform property taxes rapidly to address the growing needs of sustainable transitions and increased resilience. In doing so, we focus on two main factors that have been features of the literature for over a century. The first relates to linking the tax to local services and can be traced back to Alfred Marshall and Wicksellian foundations. The second is to base the tax on occupancy rather than ownership, sidestepping the difficult issues associated with establishing "ownership," and using an approximation for values based on property size and location. This simpler administration model can be supplemented by high-tech satellite monitoring of size and location, together with an increasing familiarity with blockchain technology, even in sub-Saharan countries.

The Case for Property Taxes, the "Wicksellian Connection," and Alfred Marshall's Beneficial Property Taxes

Linkages between costs and benefits of public services encourage "efficiency" of service delivery. Breton (1996, p.3) labeled this linkage the "Wicksellian" connection:

> Wicksell (1896) and Lindahl (1919) ... recognized that if genuine links or connections were to emerge between revenue and expenditure decisions and if true demand functions were as a result to be revealed, the public (collective) provision of goods and services would be efficient.... I will henceforth call this connection the Wicksellian connection.

Alfred Marshall (1890 [1920]) was the first author to stress the potential of property tax for ensuring efficiency. His argument was based on two premises. The first is that property taxes are beneficial when they are used to finance services that provide corresponding benefits. When services are not provided, the tax becomes "onerous." Secondly, local governments are better suited to provide services of value because of their proximity to citizens and firms. National taxes are almost always onerous, because the national government tends not to link broad-based taxes to local public goods. In Marshall's words:

> Onerous rates are those, which yield no compensating benefit to the persons who pay them. An extreme case is that of rates devoted to paying interest on a loan incurred by a municipality for an enterprise that failed and has been abandoned. Onerous rates tend of course to drive away those persons on whom they would fall... On the other hand, beneficial or remunerative rates are those spent on lighting, draining, and other purposes; so as to supply the people who pay the rates with certain necessaries, comforts and luxuries of life, which can be provided by the local authority more cheaply than in any other way.
>
> 'Services which are preponderantly national in character' are 'generally onerous', while 'those which are preponderantly local in character generally confer upon rate-payers a direct and peculiar benefit more or less commensurate with the burden'. [1]

[1] Marshall, Alfred (1890, Appendix G.).

Local governments are well situated to achieve global efficiency through the provision of local public/semipublic goods targeted to subsets of the total national population. A property tax financing (part of) these goods is important in achieving efficiency, since the consumption of the local goods affects the utility that owners/occupiers derive from property.

Vickrey (1963) has pioneered the modern literature analysis of the linkages between benefits and costs of specific local services, while Bird and Slack (2014) analyze how assignment of functions and taxes can be geared to leverage the Wicksellian connection.

The modern literature develops the theory of the capitalization of property tax (see Oates, 1972). Let us illustrate it with a simple example that uses the benefit-cost linkage to illustrate the differences between value-based and area-based property taxation. The investment in a new fire protection station in a metropolitan area reduces the time to reach properties, lowers risk of loss of property and life from fire, and provides utility to the individuals in the catchment area that decreases with distance from the station. Property owners or occupiers benefitting from the new station are ready to pay a higher price for housing in that area than for dwellings with similar characteristics with less easy access to the station. If demand exceeds the available housing in the area, it bids up property prices and determines capitalization. The theory of capitalization assumes that the value of property and its variations is the best variable to measure the benefits and to establish the link with cost of services.

The main problems with the ownership-valuation model apply largely to the recurrent property tax that is the core of the local government finances in many G7 countries, for example, the US. These relate (1) to the political economy of enforcing "onerous" tax changes on potentially asset rich but fixed-income or poor households, (2) combined with the difficulty of establishing ownership in many countries with overlapping leaseholds (including the UK), as well as (3) administrative complexity, that is often binding in stretched local governments in emerging market countries. As we see in Chap. 1, the performance of the valuation-based property tax in emerging market countries, like India and Mexico, has been pessimal—not raising more than 0.25% of GDP, or a tenth of the levels in more advanced G7 countries.

The problems enumerated above do not apply with the same intensity with respect to business properties that are subject to considerable turnover and for which market-based valuations are appropriate. Political economy constraints to taxing such properties are less binding—although in some countries the owners are well-connected and enjoy considerable political leverage. Taxing the easily identifiable assets of wealthy traders is a critical element in establishing a fully functioning income tax, especially since such people tend to be among the hard-to-tax groups.

Land Value Capture

Another feature of the theoretical case for capitalization of property taxes, popularized by multilateral agencies as the land value capture (LVC) model, is to leverage the potential increase in property values to finance investments such as metro stations, as in many G7 countries, especially the US. The automatic increases in property tax revenues as property prices increase in the metro station catchment areas facilitate levying a "betterment" tax or levy. The betterment levy presupposes that there is a functioning value-based property tax in place, so that the increments in value linked to the specific investments are identified and taxed. This is not easy to implement in most emerging market countries, where the value-based property tax has not performed at the level of some advanced G7 countries. Another LVC financing mechanism is the sale of public land to private developers, who then carry out the developments of infrastructure, often in the form of public-private partnerships. The land sale model has been used extensively in East Asia, including in China.

The relative success of the LVC model in financing infrastructure in the G7 countries especially in the US and Japan, and the opportunities it offers, explains its advocacy by multilateral agencies and academics in a range of emerging market countries. But the market discipline and monitoring of windfall gains and possible political influence are hard to replicate in most emerging market countries. In some South Asian cities, land sales based LVC is tantamount to "land grab" by well-connected interest groups or individuals, with the expulsion of poorer households often with traditional, or less well-defined or protected property rights, to increasingly distant or "informal" slums. The prevention of enforced sales at well below market prices, as in Japan, is not assured in many other cases, including in China (Wang, Wu and Ye, 2018).

Chinese local governments have increasingly relied on the land sales model of LVC since the 1993/4 reforms that began a recentralization of tax instruments and administration. This also enabled them to get around restrictions on borrowing and access to private finance, by setting up "independent" Investment Corporations and Financing Vehicles that were able to partner with private developers to finance and build local infrastructure. This model, however, led to continued urban sprawl, loss of prime agricultural land and wetlands, congestion and pollution in mega metropolises, and buildup of poorly documented off-budget liabilities, with public-private partnerships with the property developers.

After two decades of breakneck investments and exponential growth in the coastal metropolises, the difficulties with the land sales model came to a head in 2021 with the financial difficulties of several large developers (including Evergrande). The developers had relied on a continuing supply of cheap land to build on, regardless of effective demand, in an effective Ponzi-type operation. As the Chinese government clamped down on the financial requirements (three red lines) and limited land sales, the land sales model began to unwind. This has led to a major effort to shift to a proper tax-based financing arrangement for local governments.

Area-Based Taxation

An area-based property tax can be more effective than the valuation model in both generating incentives to renovate properties (e.g., to include better fire proofing in the case above) and addressing the cost of services (e.g., fire services for larger and more distant properties). Thus, size/area/location-based property taxes are better able to capture, in many cases, the costs of service delivery. This also applies to education and health care, where larger-sized properties are associated with larger families, and location introduces an element of redistribution. Benefits from health and education are connected not with market value of properties, but with the number of residents, hence correlated with property size. Also, benefits are linked to the accessibility to services, hence to the location. Indeed, the size/area/location combination is relatively simple to assess and can be made to approximate the theoretical "ideal" valuations.

While an area-based property tax is simpler to administer than the valuation alternative, the tax rates tend to be sticky and could fall behind property price changes over time. As seen in some Indian cities that have had some initial success with area-based property taxes, such as Bengaluru, adjusting rates with the opening of a new airport has not been easy, and the political economy problems inherent in the valuation model remain in the area-based iteration if the benefit linkage is not made explicit.

Making a Beneficial Recurrent Property Tax Work

A key element in making a property tax "beneficial" is the explicit linkage with basic services. This can address the political economy constraints that so concerned Alfred Marshall and generate local accountability for assigned public services.

A shift from the ownership basis of taxation to occupancy (but levied on ownership in case the property is vacant) permits the local administration to sidestep the difficult issues associated with cadaster and registration. It also makes sense to make the occupiers who benefit from the local services responsible for the benefit-linked tax. All sales would be subject to market valuations, and business properties should continue to operate under the valuation-ownership property tax. This is the current practice in the UK and many other countries.

Despite concerns that an area/location-based tax might be regressive, simulations for China and Mexico (see relevant chapters below) illustrate that a beneficial property tax with explicit linkage with basic services is likely to be equality enhancing. Also, using city per capita income as a proxy for the cost of services, the tax is much higher in more developed metropolitan areas than in smaller and more remote cities. This is likely to influence the incentives to migrate from the sprawling metropolitan areas to cleaner, more compact cities, provided that adequate employment opportunities are created. Attracting firms equally depends on the effectiveness of local infrastructure as well as connectivity with domestic or external value chains. This has given rise to the idea of a "compact, clean and connected" (CCC) city as a key element of adaptation to sustainable and inclusive growth.

A beneficial property tax could be calibrated to replace land sales in China very quickly—or raise around 2% of city/provincial GDP. In a unitary multilevel state, tax rate bands could be legislated by the central legislature, with the province or local government choosing a rate within the band. In China, this already is the practice regarding property tax sales. This makes the tax an example of own-source revenues, although sales volumes are variable. Simulations for Mexico incorporated lower revenue targets—but yielded similar results with equity that increases with the linkage to benefits and basic social spending.

An essential component of a strengthened property tax system is an accompanying equalization system, given the wide variance in tax bases as well as costs and access to public services. This is essential to ensure similar levels of public service at similar levels of tax effort to avoid widening spatial disparities and incentives to migrate to the sprawling metropolitan areas.

Administering a Property Tax

Much of the difficulty in administering property taxes lies in (1) establishing ownership and (2) the complexity of accurate valuation, in addition to the political economy difficulties in implementation, which we have outlined above.

The shift to an occupancy basis for taxation rather than ownership sidesteps the first difficulty, although for legal and spatial planning purposes and property sales a cadaster is still likely to be needed. As seen in Tanzania, it is possible to use a combination of high-tech satellite imagery, that is available even in sub-Saharan Africa, together with low-tech door-to-door verification of the nature of the properties and to determine whether the property is rented out, owner-occupied, or vacant. This also helps to establish location and size even with high-rise buildings.

The size and location basis rather than valuation also considerably simplifies administration. The linkage between rate setting and local services puts greater pressure on linking local tax rates (e.g., by sub-divisions within cities or metro areas) and establishing budget priorities. At the same time, this should also help in establishing greater local accountability for spending and outcomes.

We also examine the possible use of blockchain information for simplification of both the revenue and spending circuits and facilitation for information exchanges within government departments at the local level, with the national/state authorities, and the public. A major reformulation of governance and information management is possible, even in the less advanced countries in sub-Saharan Africa, but is certainly practicable in China, the major countries in Southeast and South Asia, the Middle East, and Latin America. Additional country-specific work is likely to be needed.

Structure of the Volume

Chapter 1 addresses the types of property taxes, provides some international examples, and discusses revenue potential. Chapter 2 looks in detail at the failures and promise of property taxation in Senegal. Chapter 3 continues the sub-Saharan African focus by examining Tanzania, with some interesting experimentation with modern satellite imagery. Chapter 4 looks at the problem of sustainable financing of local operations in China, the failure of the valuation-ownership model experiments, and the need for a beneficial property tax. The chapter also examines the overall context and need for a within-province equalization system to better anchor a beneficial property tax. Chapter 5 outlines the poor performance of the ownership-valuation property tax and betterment levy model in "federal" Mexico, growing spatial inequalities in service delivery. Simulations for a beneficial property tax illustrate similar results as in "unitary" China, and the need for a new tax to be accompanied by equalization enforcing adjustments in the revenue-sharing mechanisms. Chapter 6 addresses some of the new issues arising with administration, including combinations of high-tech satellite imagery combined with relatively simple door-to-door verification, as well as the potential for blockchains applications. Chapter 7 concludes with suggestions for policy makers in emerging market countries and areas for further investigation.

References

Bird R. and Slack E., (2014) Local Taxes And Local Expenditures In Developing Countries: Strengthening The Wicksellian Connection. Public Administration and Development. wileyonlinelibrary.com. DOI: 10.1002/pad.1695

Lindahl E., (1919) Just taxation – A positive solution. In Classics in Musgrave R, Peacock A (eds) The Theory of Public Finance. Macmillan: London, 1964; 85–98.

Marshall A., (1890) Principles of Economics (8th ed.), Macmillan & Co. Appendix G. Edition used: Principles of Economics. Macmillan and Co., London (8th ed. 1920), Online Library of Liberty.

Oates W., (1972) Fiscal Federalism. Harcourt Brace Jovanovich, New York

Vickrey W., (1963) General and specific financing of urban services. In Public Expenditure Decisions in the Urban Community. In Schaller H (ed) Resources for the Future: Washington; 62–90.

Wang W, Wu A and Ye F I (2018) "Land use reforms: towards sustainable development in China," in Ahmad, Niu and Xiao (eds) op cit.

Wicksell K, (1896) A new principle of just taxation. In Classics in the Theory of Public Finance, Musgrave R, Peacock A (eds). Macmillan: London, 1964; 72–118.

CHAPTER 1

Property Taxation, Instruments, Models, Administration, and Potential Effects

Abstract There are several alternative design issues related to property taxation, problems with administration and rent-seeking, and diverse international experiences. A taxonomy distinguishes between recurrent and non-recurrent taxes, on households and businesses. The predominant value and ownership-based approach relies on recording of ownership and timely integration of current market prices. Cadasters are the bedrock for this model. However, recording of ownership, and updating values is a very lengthy and costly activity, particularly in developing and transition countries where property rights are hard to define, with huge informality and areas with collective ownership. Collections show a dismal performance, especially with the old colonial model relying on tax collectors that interface directly with taxpayers. An alternative is based in area/location-based taxes using easily verifiable parameters. Together with basing taxation on occupancy rather than ownership, the alternative simplifies recurrent taxation on households. But the political economy problem of taxing fixed-income households according to variations in prices is a significant constraint. This can be addressed by an explicit linkage with local benefits—and leads to better accountability and better access to public services, including for the informal sector. International experiences and revenue potential are also addressed in this chapter.

Keywords Taxonomy of property taxes • Value-based models • Area-based models • Revenue potential

E. Ahmad, G. Brosio, *Beneficial Property Taxation for Emerging Market Countries*, https://doi.org/10.1007/978-3-031-08612-0_1

1 Typology of Property Taxation

A distinction should usefully be made in relation to the recurrent taxation of residential properties and business properties (i.e., land and buildings separately, typically on a yearly basis), and non-recurrent taxation of sales or bequests (inheritance/gifts), or additions to values as a result of public investments (e.g., betterment levies). See Table 1.1 for a summary.

Table 1.1 Typology of instruments for property taxation

	Recurrent taxes (yearly)	*Non-recurrent taxes*			
	Property tax/ land tax	*Registration/ stamp duties*	*VAT*	*Capital gains tax*	*Betterment levies*
Who is liable for tax and when?	a) Owners b) Occupiers	Sale/transfer for consideration, or free	Sale of new property	Increase of value between points of times	Increase of value deriving from public infrastructure projects
Tax base	a. Value of land only b. Value of buildings only c. Value of land plus buildings d. Physical size and location of property	Value of transaction	Value of transaction	Difference between present and initial values	Difference between values after and before project
Taxpayer	Owner/ occupant	Buyer	Seller	Owner	Owner
Defining the tax base	1. Assessment of market value 2. Parameters linked to size/location	Price of property at sale	Price of property at sale	Assessment of market values	Assessment of market values

Source: Ahmad et al. (2018)

1.1 Recurrent Property Taxation

There are typically two broad options for taxing residential properties on a recurrent basis: the US-centric ownership/valuation model requires accurate information usually from updated cadasters, and alternatives based on simpler but more robust mechanisms such as size and location of the property. These can also be made to approximate valuation changes. Political-economy constraints are addressed in the second model through a direct linkage with basic services, and the adjustment in the delivery/cost of these services is a useful approximation to the adjustments needed in the valuation-ownership model. The benefit linkages make for a "beneficial tax."

In most emerging market economies, a US-style property tax (based on ownership and valuation) has not had much success. Note that such a tax was abandoned in the UK in the early 1990s for residential property (but not for business properties). Variants experimented in China, for example, in Shanghai and Chongqing, were not very successful—largely because of relatively complex ownership and leasehold patterns and difficulties with valuations, as well as the constraints posed by imposing market-based taxation on fixed-income households living in potentially expensive areas.

The biggest drawback to the introduction of a valuations-based property tax is that potentially asset-rich households on fixed incomes or pensions would not be able to pay the tax, especially in the case of sudden increases, even when they are backed by increases in property values. They also tend to lack the support networks to be able to move to "cheaper cities."

Recurrent taxes can be levied on land only (empty land), or on built-on land, meaning land plus buildings. In the case of built-up land, the value of buildings must be separated from the value of the land, and this is a very complex task.

A small number of countries tax land only, using a land tax. This may also apply in rural areas. In developing countries, land is used mostly for agriculture, making a tax on land mostly a tax on agricultural land (see Ahmad and Stern 1991, for a discussion of the rural land tax pertaining to South Asia).

In many countries, taxes are levied on the combined value of buildings and the land on which they are located, popularly referred to as the property tax. Most countries, particularly the industrial countries, levy a tax that includes *de jure* in the tax base both all empty land and built-up land. De facto, only built-up land and empty land in the urban areas are taxed.

There is typically a stronger market for commercial property than residential property, given that there is usually a denser network of such transactions. Thus, a recurrent property tax on businesses based on valuations should work well. In such cases, also the fixed-income argument against the valuation-ownership model does not apply as strongly as with housing. This instrument should also form the basis for betterment levies on businesses, an important source for financing connectivity infrastructure (see, e.g., the financing for Crossrail, the biggest infrastructure investment in the UK in the past decades, Ahmad et al. 2019, London School of Economics/Coalition for Urban Transition (LSE/CUT)).

1.2 Non-recurrent Taxation

Although non-recurrent property taxation may in some cases generate substantial revenues, the fact of the matter is that property transactions are not uniformly spaced over time and do not assure local governments of a secure revenue source. We discuss below the special case of land sales that has been so influential as a source of financing local infrastructure in China, particularly along the East Coast.

There are two non-recurrent selective instruments targeted to tax only variations in the value of property. These are the tax on capital gains and betterment taxes aimed at capturing the increase in value derived from public infrastructure work.[1] The latter is one component of the popular notion of "land value capture" that inter alia also includes land sales.

Taxes on transfer of property are frequently called registration or stamp taxes or duties and exist in almost all countries. Also, capital gains taxes are frequently used and share with transfer taxes the tax base and, for residential properties, the moment when they are levied. They are important for their revenue potential and relative ease of administration. There are also political economy, revenue, and distributional objectives that govern the use of these taxes, such as the Stamp Duties on Land Transactions in England. Experts argue frequently against such taxation on the grounds that these cause distortions in the immovable property and labor markets. In practice, there may even be distributional and revenue advantages, as in the UK, where significant revenues are generated by higher stamp duties on expensive properties, for example, mainly in London. This also has the

[1] Good summaries are provided by Bahl and Wallace (2008); Mirrlees Report (2011); Norregaard (2013).

advantage of discouraging migration to the crowded Greater London metropolitan area.

First sales are typically subjected to the value added tax (VAT). This is designed to reduce the cost of construction as developers can offset the VAT on purchases of cement and steel and other products against the VAT on sales. Furthermore, this brings the transactions of the construction sector within the purview of the tax administration and reduces the prospects that funds can be misappropriated, as is the case in many countries.

As a result, we can conceive of two main, not mutually exclusive instruments: the property tax targeted for the urban areas and the land tax for rural areas. There are frequent overlaps between these, especially as the formal delineation of urban jurisdictions lag the actual urban sprawl in many cities.

2 Defining the Recurrent Property Tax Base—Value or Area/Location

We focus initially on recurrent taxes on household property. We first identify the main types of value-based taxation, and then the area-based alternatives.

2.1 Value-Based Taxes

There are several variants where the tax base is valued in money terms. Methods of valuation differ. The capital value of land and improvements involving buildings is identified in most countries by the market value. However, identifying the market value of properties presents a challenging problem in implementing a property tax in developing countries, given the more limited number of market transactions than for businesses (see Bahl and Wallace 2008).

Complications arise when countries try to separately tax the value of land, and then the value of buildings or improvements to built-up structures. Although theoretically attractive, these combinations have proved difficult to implement given limitations on the number of surveyors in most developing countries.

For these variants the aim of the tax administration is to approximate as much as possible the current market prices. Approximation, that is, the determination of the tax base, is done according to two approaches. First, economic modeling could be used in countries with sophisticated administrations. Hedonic models of real estate are used to replicate market prices observed from the actual sales of a representative sample of properties. The estimated implicit market prices of property characteristics are then used for the determination of the value, approximating the market price of all properties. The hedonic pricing method is based on realization that prices of goods in a market are affected by their characteristics. For example, the price of an individual parking lot will depend on its location, its accessibility, umbrage, and so on. So, this method helps us to estimate the value of a commodity, or an asset, based on people's willingness to pay for the commodity or asset as and when its characteristics change.[2] This approach is referred to as the computer-assisted mass appraisal (CAMA) method and is used presently in many countries, and by cadastral agencies.

The second approach, or the traditional cadastral method, is based on the expertise of surveyors and tax officials. Property values are assessed individually applying to the reference unit price of property several parameters representing the relevant characteristics of the concerned property.

Both approaches require detailed information on all the characteristics of properties impacting the price. In the literature, a distinction is made between structural characteristics, such as age, maintenance, quality of the materials, and variables reflecting location and access to services.

Tracking Ownership and Values

The typical model of property taxation used in industrial countries and followed in most emerging market economies is based on ownership, as in

[2] The computer assisted mass assessment (CAMA) method approximates market price (AMP) based on hedonic prices. It consists of two steps.

The first step provides the estimation of the hedonic model

$P_i = (s_i S_i, l_i L_i)$

where:

P_i is the market price observed at sale for a random sample of properties

S_i is a vector of characteristics of the structural characteristics of the property

L_i is a vector of characteristics related to the location of properties

s_i and l_i are the estimated coefficients associated with the characteristics; usually interpreted as the implicit marginal prices for the characteristics.

The second step approximates the price of property *i* and of the tax due:

$AMP_i = \Sigma\, s_i \boldsymbol{S}_i + l_i \boldsymbol{L}_i$

where:

$\boldsymbol{S}_i$ and $\boldsymbol{L}_i$ are the actual values of the characteristics of property *i*

$Tax_1 = t_i AMP_i$

the US, Canada, and many European countries, **or** alternatively on occupancy of properties, as in the UK, or both, as in France, and on an accurate valuation mechanism. To make the model fully operational, there needs to be an accurate record of the property, as well as ownership/or occupancy, and changes in prices and valuations. Records of properties, ownership, and values are typically kept in cadasters.

Market forces drive valuations and there is typically timely and accurate information on property values and sales, tracked both by the market as well as the (local) tax administrations. In principle, (yardstick) competition limits both tax rates and burdens as well as the level and quality of public services. Improvements in infrastructure—for example, opening of a new metro line or stop—are immediately reflected in property values, hence taxes, and affect the local government's ability to issue bonds or borrow for the improvements in infrastructure.

Property prices are closely linked to quality of public schools and effectiveness of local services. If these services are not provided effectively, people move with their feet to a jurisdiction that provides better quality services (particularly education in the US). This has an important feedback effect on property values and taxes, as well as the income tax base. The resulting fiscal pressures are part of the electoral discipline that comes about with yardstick competition.

While this model is appealing in many respects, its adoption faces huge challenges in many emerging market and developing countries (as well as some Organization for Economic Cooperation and Development (OECD) countries—the UK example is discussed below). There are several layers of difficulty with this model, and we explore them sequentially and suggest ways for its better adaptation to the prevailing context of emerging market and developing countries.

Cadasters or Registers with Complex Ownership Patterns

Maintaining cadasters is the bedrock of property management systems. However, maintaining cadasters and keeping them up to date is typically a difficult, complex, and costly task. The situation is made more complex in many emerging countries with widespread state or communal land, and migrations leading to "informal" settlements, especially in the environs of large metropolitan areas (Dar es Salaam) or capital cities (Dakar or Mexico City).

In many developing and emerging market countries, little is known about what properties are located and where. This applies equally to low-end informal properties, as well as to high-end properties as farms and single properties are torn down and replaced by luxury condominiums. In many metropolitan areas in Africa (e.g., Cairo) and in Asia, only properties within the physical limits of the old cities are classified as urban, and many new satellite towns and high-end suburbs remain zoned as rural.

Often there is an overlap between state ownership and traditional or communal property rights that have not been extinguished. In many countries with state ownership of land, as in China, or long-standing hereditary ownership by nobles, as in the UK, leaseholds of various lengths have evolved. This provides limited rights of alienation of property in England subject to subinfeudation. This mechanism is also used in Tanzania, where foreigners are permitted to "own" properties on alienable 98-year leases.

The multiple and often overlapping property rights complicate the ownership-valuation model. An immediate consequence is the mushrooming of informal settlements with substandard living conditions and poor access to public services in and around major cities. Particularly damaging is the absence of incentives to improve the "uncertain" living conditions, together with the inability to access credit. This has deleterious long-term effects on the quality of life of an increasing and mostly vulnerable segment of the population and on meeting the Sustainable Development Goals (SDG) targets.

Difficulties of Recurrent Property Taxation: Valuation

Valuation is the most difficult administration task and is hugely problematic in many developing and emerging market economies. It is often not clear what buildings or additions are constructed relative to the legacy cadasters. Similarly, it is hard to incorporate the effects of additional improvements (e.g., metro stops or road and other infrastructure investments) on market prices.

One of the principal difficulties with valuation and changes in valuation is that markets in developing countries do not operate with the efficiency as in advanced industrial countries. Furthermore, the information base is much more segmented, severely curtailing the relevance of the typical property tax model found in advanced countries for emerging market countries.

The distributional advantages of property taxation disappear when high-end properties and improvements are effectively excluded from the tax base.

2.2 *Area-Based Approaches*

The second alternative for the definition of the property tax base is the area-based approach. The crucial factor for determining the tax base is the physical size and area of properties. There are various alternatives in the area-based approach, from the simplest to the most ambitious.

Area Only

The tax due is determined, very simply (as in the case of specific taxes, such as excises), by multiplying a measure of the tax base (e.g., square meters) by the tax rate expressed in money units (i.e., dollars per square meter).[3] Mauritius used this model from 1995 to 2010, with the central government levying the National Residential Property Tax. Collections were very modest because of the very low tax rate applied and huge non-compliance. Real property was taxed by local governments also with a value-based tax, limiting the room for a centrally levied tax. The main attraction of this type of tax is the simplicity of assessment (although the precise calculation of square meters is not as easy as one could imagine) and that new buildings can be immediately taxed after completion. Again, completion is not easy to assess as owners tend to delay updating, precisely to avoid taxation, as we can observe in emerging but also industrialized countries (see Fig. 1.1 from Italy).

Area and Location

The addition of location improves the efficiency of the area-based tax, introducing a link between its burden and the publicly provided services. As a matter of fact, location in an urban setting reflects the impact of government policies on the value of property and on the welfare of occupants.

[3] The area-based approach has two variants. First, the tax base can be determined in physical terms

$Tax_1 = m^2 T_i$

where:

Tax_1 is the tax due on property *I*; m^2 is number of square meters; T_i is the tax rate (in money units).

In the second variant the tax base is expressed in money terms.

$Tax_1 = m^2\, SMRP\, t_i$

where,

SMRP is the reference price of a square meter of property:

t_i is the tax rate in percentage terms.

Fig. 1.1 Red peppers hanging from an unfinished house in Calabria

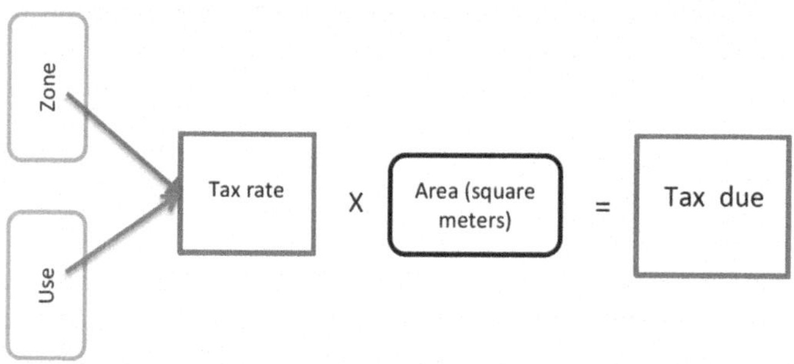

Fig. 1.2 Working of an area-based tax

It is of course possible to refine area-based assessments including factors such as quality of housing, as well as the age or type of property (apartment, single-family houses, villas, etc.). Figure 1.2 that follows provides a graphical illustration of the application of the tax. The tax, in this example, is determined according to three variables. Two of them, in this case zone, that is, location, and use, modify the tax rate (expressed in units of dollars). The weighed tax rate is then multiplied by the area to obtain the tax liability. Alternatively, location and use could be placed in the formula after the area, leading to a weighed area. Taxes using a weighted notion of area to determine the tax base are called "area-based taxes" (see Ahmad et al. 2018), "parametric taxes," or also "point-based taxes" (Collier et al. 2018).

It is important to note that, as the number of factors/parameters applied to area increases, the tax base calculated with this method comes closer to the tax base estimated by cadasters.[4] Increasing complexity of the process, however, leads to greater discretion on the part of local tax officials and opens the gates to rent-seeking behavior. It does not guarantee that the area-based tax will be a "beneficial tax" and the political economy difficulties of adjusting the tax remain.

Despite their simplicity, area-based taxes can be quite productive in terms of revenue. There is no a priori reason why they should be inferior to value-based taxes. The decisive factors for determining revenue their productivity are the tax rate and tax administration. Israel's Arnona (see OECD 2021) is a good example of productivity, generating 1.9% of GDP. It is also to be noted that residential properties contribute to more than the half of total collections of Arnona.[5]

The Mauritius National Residential Property Tax (NRPT) collected by the central government until 2010, contributed to a mere 0.003% of total national collections. The NRPT was assessed only against square meters, while Arnona weighs them with other factors. But NRPT charged the equivalent of US$1,05 (Rupees 30) per square meter of floor area (Olima 2010),[6] while Arnona charges on average the equivalent of US$8,76 (NIS 29,2) per square meter.[7]

[4] Cadasters calculate the tax by determining the tax base according to a formula of the following type $Tax\ base = m2\ SMRPa_i$

where:

a_i is a vector of coefficients applied to the reference price of a square meter (Smrp). Coefficients are determined by cadastral officers, or surveyors.

The tax due is then: $Tax_1 = t_i SMRPa_i$

The difference between an area-based model and a cadaster model disappears as the number of coefficients used to weigh the Smrp equals the number of coefficients included in the a_i vector.

[5] https://jerusaleminstitute.org.il/en/blog/arnona-by-use-in-israel/

[6] Washington H. A. Olima, Property Taxation in Anglophone East Africa: Case Study of Mauritius 2010 Lincoln Institute of Land Policy.

[7] Israel's Arnona does not provide a good example with respect to transparency, however: "information on each parcel of property, such as size, age, and Arnona charge is neither publicly available, nor reported to the Ministry of Finance and/or the Ministry of the Interior" (OECD 2021, p. 69).

The standard Indian property tax is based on the "ownership and valuation model" common in Western countries. The valuation is based on an estimate of the annual rental or capital value of the property (Valuation (Metropolis) Act of 1869). However, as pointed out in Bird and Rao (2012), the information base on the property tax in India is severely deficient and unreliable. This is partly because the cadaster is woefully out of date, and the valuation system has not kept pace with market price changes.

A number of Indian cities use a relatively complex version of area-based property tax, where the tax rate is supposed to measure the average value of property per square meter. This tax rate is weighed with other factors to adjust to the variability in property prices and then multiplied by the number of square meters. Cities using this model, shown in bold in Table 1.2, such as Bengaluru and Hyderabad, do not perform worse than cities using the value-based approach (in black ink) and the overall revenue collections remain poor at less than 0.25% of GDP after over a century of implementation. The idea, as in Pune, Delhi, Bengaluru, and Surat, was to move to

Table 1.2 Indian property tax collections per capita by city 2015–6 (Rs. per capita). Area-based implementation in Italics

1. Pune	2676
2. Visakhapatnam	2059
3. Bengaluru	*2053*
4. Hyderabad	*1686*
5. Chennai	1224
6. Mumbai	1121
7. Ahmedabad	804
8. Lucknow	714
9. Delhi	*705*
10. Bhopal	477
11. Thiruvananthapuram	469
12. Ludhiana	376
13. Raipur	311
14. Bhubaneshwar	256
15. Patna	*193*
16. Chandigarh	182
17. Dehradun	141
18. Ranchi	109
19. Kanpur	64
20. Jaipur	7

Source: Awasthi Rajul and Mohan Nagarajan (2020). Original sources: City Budget statement for FY16 for all cities. Financials except Raipur; City Financial Statements for FY16 for Raipur

a presumptive basis for taxing properties based on location and size to try to approximate true values, and to simplify and minimize the contact between the local tax administrators and the taxpayers. The arms' length arrangement was to minimize opportunities for rent-seeking and corruption. This reform was initiated in Patna in 1992/3 but failed to yield significant additional revenues. A similar outcome occurred in Delhi. However, in Bengaluru, the application of presumptive estimates led to a virtual doubling of the property tax revenues between 2007/8 and 2008/9 (Bird and Rao 2012).

The typical problems with arbitrary adjustments to presumptive measures have appeared recently in Bengaluru. A 40% increase in valuations due to the new airport led to inequities within Bengaluru and had to be rescinded—and increases were capped at 25%. Fine-tuning the valuations to specific neighborhoods, as well as a use of bands linked to the cost-of-service delivery, might yield more accurate changes and less political resistance. This would also enhance the effective accountability of the third tier of government that has been assured legally with a Constitutional amendment. More recent attempts to link components of the property tax to key public services through an earmarked "cess" move Bengaluru's property tax system toward a "beneficial model." These are discussed further below.

With an area/location-based tax, the tax liability is determined through the application of a unit tariff (e.g., *n* dollars) to indicators or parameters of property size and value of use.[8]

Self-declaration of parameters by taxpayers, ***largely applied around the world for the main taxes,*** circumvents problems of information and administration capacity. It makes the area-based tax a viable solution for most emerging and developing countries.

An area-based tax can be adapted to the local circumstances, choosing the model according to the availability of information and capacity.

- It can be implemented quickly with satellite technology, together with very simple verification and registration mechanisms.

[8] A typical basic formula would be: $Tax\ due = n\ X\ m^2$, where n is the unit tariff, let's say 10 Euros, and m^2 is number of square meters.

- To the extent that it begins to tax high-end properties, this would be an improvement over the un-implementable ownership-valuation model that either misses out or undervalues high-end properties.
- Taxpayers' resistance would be addressed if the tax were linked to the provision of basic local services—enhancing accountability and meeting the SDGs more effectively.

2.3 *Comparing the Models*

Economic Efficiency
Efficiency in taxation involves evaluating the impact of taxes on their base. Any increase of a tax reduces its tax base, when the tax is not shifted elsewhere, because its use becomes more expensive. This stimulates a more efficient use of the tax base. Area-based taxes achieve higher economic efficiency compared with value-based taxes. This is because they promote efficient use of space, stimulating the use of small residential and commercial units and a more efficient use of their space. This is of particular importance in crowded urban areas.

Administration Costs
The costs of administrating an area-based property tax system are clearly lower than the costs of administrating a value-based system. This latter system requires the creation, maintenance, and continuous updating of a fiscal cadaster, a very costly operation. Area-based models demand simply the keeping of a registry of properties, with names of owners or occupants, size of property, and its location (zone). More complex variants of the model require additional information than can be provided by the taxpayers through self-declaration. Self-declaration is more in tune with the logic of an area-based tax than a value-based tax, as we will observe later in this volume.

Pure administrative costs such as the sending out of tax bills, and efforts involved in collecting taxes from delinquent taxpayers would be the same with the two systems.

Growth of Revenue
Costs of providing public services generally rise over time in money terms. This applies particularly to local services due to their large labor input, indicating that the desired trend for local taxes is a steady growth of

collections in keeping with service delivery costs, and not necessarily changes in property values. In the practice the two models work in the same way, since most countries adopt a (mostly) yearly coefficient of adjustment, usually the year-to-year increase in the cost of living to the previous year's tax due. This implies that most countries tend to ignore the change in the tax base and proceed to its updating only at very long intervals. For example, the UK did not update individual values until the introduction of the Council Tax in 1993. France, Germany, and Italy have not updated in the last 40 years.

Area-based models create relatively few problems with updating. Size and benefits from locations vary smoothly over time, being relatively shielded from fluctuations in the overall economy. These are easy to assess and annual links with the cost of living can ensure steady growth and would be politically acceptable, if done continuously. Governments are inclined to skip election years, however.

The logic of value-based models requires continuous updating of individual values to ensure fairness of treatment. This is costly to perform, even with modern systems of computerized mass assessments. This is because they must be fed with information about changes in all the characteristics of property that are used in the assessment of values. As mentioned above, governments tend to greatly delay the updating, which in turn, with the passing of time, becomes politically more unpalatable, because of the increasing gaps between market prices and assessed values. As time passes gaps between the market values and across the board updated values gets wider. This increases the perceived unfairness of the tax for those taxpayers whose property price is lagging below the adjustment index.

Transparency/Obfuscation

Area-based property taxes are structurally a simple and transparent tax instrument. The tax due depends only on a very few and easy-to-measure factors, such as physical size area, location, and type of use. Obviously, complexity and obfuscation arise when governments attempt to increase the equity or other aims of the tax and add additional factors to the formula. Transparency does not arise by itself, but it rather results from government policies. It requires taxpayers' free access to all data and information used for calculating the tax due.

Self-declaration approaches have a built-in higher degree of transparency but could be misleading without penalties for mis-declarations. While both Bengaluru and Bogotá had significant revenue gains with the introduction of self-declaration of property values and characteristics. However, over time it became increasingly difficult to ensure that the declared valuations accurately tracked actual changes—and the political economy constraints of fixed-income or low-income households unable to fully reflect property price adjustments in their declarations emerged as a major constraint given the large number of households involved.

Equity

In most developed countries, the income tax is the most effective redistribution instrument available if it effectively tracks the income distribution and there is an exemption limit. Almost by definition the income tax is more progressive than a property tax. This pattern is seen for Canada in Table 1.3. The first, poorer quintile, for example, has a share of income, 6.7% of the total, that is half of its share of property, while the richest one has a share of income that is higher than the share of market value. Most countries try to correct the regressivity of the tax. Canada grants exemptions to lower-income property taxpayers.

In many developing countries, however, the income tax largely covers formal sector wages, and non-wage income (including from property and financial assets) is hard to track, and often favorably treated, making the income tax much less progressive, if not regressive. Whether or not it is progressive than a property tax becomes a moot point, especially if high-end properties are not properly valued.

Under these circumstances, accurately measuring properties' size and location provides considerable information to the income tax authorities

Table 1.3 Canada: shares by quintiles of after-tax personal income and property market value, 1999

	Median after-tax income	*Share of after-tax income*	*Share of market value of property*
Quintile	$	%	
Lowest	18,300	6.7	14.9
Second	31,300	12.7	16.8
Third	43,500	17.6	18.1
Fourth	58,300	23.7	21.4
Highest	85,100	39.3	28.8

Source; Palameta and Macredie 2005

that can then separately track sales on a valuation basis to also the level of income taxes. Thus, there is a close relationship between information on property, and property sales, and the income tax that should be taken into consideration when assessing equity. Property is an important component of the ability to pay and taxing both income and property increases the overall equity of taxation.[9]

Most importantly, in a decentralized context, taxes are assigned to local government to finance basic services and not primarily to correct wealth and income distributions. Equity issues then turn to the combined effect of tax and expenditure at the local level. If local authorities implement policies that favor relatively more occupants of poor properties, the progressivity of the expenditure will correct the regressive character of the revenue. More specifically, the capitalization of the expenditure can have a larger impact on values of property than the capitalization of the tax. As we see from the simulations for both China and Mexico, a beneficial property tax linked to local services in most cases is progressive.

To the extent that basic services and access to credit for local public investments are a function of local own-source revenues, the issue of the effects of the property tax on equity cannot be addressed without consideration of whether additional and sustainable employment generation emerges over the medium term.

3 Dismal Revenue Collections from the Property Tax in Emerging Market Countries

There is a dismal overall collection of revenues from property taxes in developing economies, with collections well below 1% of GDP in most countries (except South Africa, and for a short period, Mauritius). It is not easy to put together consistent data on property taxation, comparable across countries. As illustrated by the Senegalese example (see Chap. 2 in this volume), actual collections in many sub-national jurisdictions might not be known in many emerging market countries, including for the national governments. While there are international standards for recording the requisite information, such as the International Monetary Fund

[9] The simple example considers two individuals with same taxable income, the first of them having only income from labor and the second one having income from wealth and income from labor. Taxing only income will not reflect the second individual's greater capacity to pay deriving from security offered by property.

(IMF) Government Finance Statistics Manual 2014 (GFSM), many countries including in South Asia, do not provide general government data (for all levels of government), and the provision of information on budgetary central government misses out sub-national jurisdictions where property taxes are typically collected, making cross-country comparison difficult. Even when roughly comparable methodologies are used, such as by the IMF and OECD, classification variations generate significant differences in, especially for non-recurrent revenues (as seen, e.g., for Argentina in Table 1.4).

The IMF's GFSM in principle makes a distinction between (1131) recurrent taxes on immovable property; (1132) recurrent taxes on net wealth; (1133) estate, inheritance, and gift taxes; (1134) taxes on financial and capital transactions; (1135) other non-recurrent taxes on property; and (1136) other recurrent taxes on property. Betterment fees and levies are included in the non-recurrent tax category. Taxes on capital gains on property are recorded as taxes on income, profits, and capital gains. However, not all countries report data on general government (including sub-national jurisdictions where most of the property taxes are levied), and the published data in the Governmental Finance Statistics Yearbook aggregate the property tax data under a single category: (113) property taxes and does not distinguish between recurrent and non-recurrent taxes on property (see Table 1.4, first panel).

The published OECD data (Table 1.4 in the second panel) makes the useful distinction between recurrent and non-recurrent taxes, but also includes movable property and the other items (1132-1136) above under the GFSM 2014 definitions in its definition. The high-income countries that best perform with respect to recurrent property taxation include Canada and the UK (at 3% of GDP), and the latter has abandoned the valuation-ownership model. The US and France have managed around 2.5% of GDP, and Israel and Japan have around 2% of GDP. The ownership-valuation model in virtually all emerging market countries has underperformed relative to potentials and levels achieved in the advanced countries.

With the perceived limited revenue potential of property taxation, relative to the main wide area taxes, such as the VAT, excises, CIT, or PIT, there is a tendency in structural reform programs to ignore or bypass discussion of both policy and administration of property taxes. Also, the standard approach to tax administration is typically that it would be a diversion for the tax administration to be concerned with a myriad of small taxpayers for relatively small revenue gains, especially since large taxpayers typically generate over three quarters of total revenue.

Table 1.4 Property tax collections (% GDP): IMF and OECD sources

IMF Government Financial Statistical Yearbooks Property Tax (#113)			*OECD Revenue Statistics*				
	2019	*2020*		*Recurrent taxes 2018*	*Recurrent taxes 2019*	*Recurrent plus non-recurrent taxes 2018*	*Recurrent plus non-recurrent taxes 2019*
Argentina	0.07	0.3	Argentina	0.4	0.4		2.6
Australia	1.63	1.61	Australia	1.7	1.7	2.7	2.7
Austria	0.21	0.23	Austria	0.2	0.2	0.5	0.5
Belgium	2.41	2.37	Belgium	1.2	1.3	3.4	3.4
Brazil	1.59	1.63	Brazil	0.7	0.7	1.4	1.5
Canada	3.76	4.05	Canada	3.1	3	3.9	3.9
China	1.41	1.32	China	0.6	0.5	1.4	1.4
Colombia	1.29	1.33	Colombia	0.8	0.8	1.5	1.8
France	3.9	3.96	France	2.5	2.4	4	3.9
Germany	0.62	0.69	Germany	0.4	0.4	1.1	1.1
Japan	2.3	2.41	Japan	1.9	1.9	2.6	2.6
Israel	1.91	1.79	Israel	1.9	1.9	3.1	3.1
Mauritius	0.1	0.09	Mexico	0.2	0.2	0.3	0.3
Mexico	0.33	0.31	Switzerland	0.2	0.2	2	2.1
Switzerland	1.86	1.96	United Kingdom	3.1	3.1	4.1	4.1
United Kingdom	3.27	3.16	USA	2.7	2.6	2.9	2.9
USA	2.96	3.12					

Source: IMF, GFS Yearbooks
Source: OECD, Revenue Statistics 2021

Determining how much revenue recurrent property taxation can potentially yield is challenging. Models, typically found in the literature, do not provide much support in examining whether a local property tax leads to underprovision or overprovision of public services, with different real outcomes depending on the approaches (Wildasin and Wilson 1991; Zodrow and Mieszkowski 1986; Zodrow 2006). While it is in principle possible to determine the size of the tax base, provided there were adequate information based on a census or surveys, there is no possible objective determination of the tax effort applicable to the exploitation of the tax base. Also, potential revenue depends on administration cost that can be extremely high with property taxation.

A less ambitious target for analysts and policy makers is to estimate the amount of revenue that can be collected by the full application of the legal requirements of the tax. Differences between actual and legal potential revenue reflect not only effort in administration, that is inefficiency in collection, but also policy choices about the effective use of legal provisions, such as primarily exemptions.

Bahl and Wallace (2008) use World Bank data on estimated values of land and property for a very large number of countries and cover both built (urban properties) and agricultural land (see Table 1.5). They estimate that potential collections from a recurrent property tax should reach between 2% and 3% of GDP. This is a high multiple of present collections in most countries. For Senegal, the exercise suggests a potential of 3% deriving mostly from agricultural land with no consideration of existing constraints (see also the estimate of 2% from IMF (2016)).

A more modest target of 1% of GDP for the property tax is simpler to achieve in most cases (China has a higher target). Brazil (albeit well below potential) and only two countries in Africa have come close—South Africa and Mauritius, and the latter also for a very short period. The Latin American average is 0.33% of GDP, with much more extensive cadasters and efficient tax administrations. Yet 1% of GDP should be a sufficient first step for whole countries, meaning higher ratios for the main metropolitan areas and for selective "growth hubs."

Table 1.5 Potential property tax revenues versus actuals for selected emerging market countries (% of GDP)

	Potential (Bahl and Wallace, 2008)	*Actual*
Argentina	2.7	0.59
Bolivia	3.2	0.40
Brazil	3.2	1.01
Chile	2.5	0.60
Colombia	4.7	0.70
Mexico	3.3	0.20
Peru	3.1	0.17
Senegal	3.0	0.10

Source: Based on Bahl and Wallace (2008) and IMF Government Finance Statistics GFS (recent years).

Metropolitan and urban areas of emerging countries have a concentration of property values that provides them a tax base that can contribute to the financing of a share of local expenditure like that of high-income countries, under the assumption of linkage with effective provision of services.

Yet, there is a growing recognition of the potential role of property taxation in the sustainable development agenda, even if the revenue potential remains relatively small in comparison with an overall target of around 18–20% of GDP for general government revenues for the Millenium Development Goals (MDG)s/SDGs (Ahmad 2015, 2017).

A system of property taxation can begin to provide information on assets. This is a significant element in moving toward more effective taxation of income and capital gains tax—which also perform badly in most emerging market economies. In the Scandinavian countries, Italy, and the US, a local/state piggy-back on the personal income tax (PIT) may be applied at the discretion of the relevant sub-national government. These supplement the accountability of the jurisdiction and its officials—but the property tax payments can generally offset the income tax liability. More importantly, information from the property tax valuations and transactions are used to cross-check income tax statements by individuals.

4 Rate Setting, Local Accountability, and Other Advantages

One of the potential advantages of a local tax system is the possible enhancement of local accountability. This comes about by the local government deciding on the rate of taxation at the margin and effectively constitutes a precondition for hard budget constraints.

Even in unitary states (like China, Tanzania, or Senegal), the essence of accountability would involve local rate setting at the margin, for example, within brackets determined by the central level. This is already the case with taxes on property transfers in China. Such a tax would constitute an own-source revenue, even if the central tax administration or another body carries out all other administrative functions. It is the setting of rates, rather than administration, that indicates whether a tax is own-source or not and whether this tax can be leveraged to access private finance through the issuance of bonds or direct borrowing.

In cases where the local governments do not set the rate or the base, as is typically the case in African and Latin American countries, the property tax revenues are no different from transfers from higher levels of administration.

The property tax is even further removed from local governments when they lack information as to how much should be, or was, collected and their share of the collections.

In addition to overall accountability, local rate setting leads to improved decision-making vis-à-vis devolved or decentralized spending responsibilities. First, own-sources of revenues permit access to credit for public investments in a sustainable manner. Second, paying taxes also facilitates household access to credit. This results in more responsible decision-making at the household and local government levels. These important effects are hard to quantify precisely, as they depend also on the institutional elements that we discuss further below.

5 Ability to Pay and Benefit Approaches and Assignment of Property Taxation

There are two alternative approaches to immovable property taxation: the ability to pay and the benefit approach. According to the first approach, property is one of the most important indicators of the ability to pay taxes and can be taxed to help in redistributing wealth. Since redistribution can be best performed at the national level, an ability to pay oriented property taxation is best assigned to the central government, as stressed by the normative theory. However, both yardstick competition and the significant advantages of local information explain why property is predominantly taxed at the local level around the world and across different institutional arrangements.

The second approach focuses on the link between the burden of the tax and the benefits received and has illustrious antecedents—starting with John Stuart Mill (1848). This is not necessarily in conflict with the ability to pay approach, given the correlation between property values and level and quality of public services. Clearly, in a perfect tax-benefit framework there is no net burden. This should make the tax more appealing to taxpayers and politicians.

The link is seen in the capitalization of the tax and benefits on property values. Most of the services capitalized in values are provided locally, making the property tax an eminently local revenue instrument. Alfred Marshall famously developed this argument by labeling local property tax as a "beneficial" tax in antithesis to "onerous" national taxes (first edition 1890; reprinted 1920). This is quite a positive view that cannot conceal the fact that the property tax is one of the most visible tax instruments. Unless the tax is clearly linked to social services or benefits, it generates political resistance (see Ahmad et al. 2015).

The linkages between tax and expenditure determine the choice of the base and formats for taxing property as a local revenue mobilization instrument. The introduction and/or reform of such an instrument requires careful consideration of a vast array of issues and requires strategic choices regarding the type of instrument used, the selection of the taxpayer, the method of administration and collection, with careful consideration of constraints, such as facilitating compliance and limiting political opposition, exploiting the revenue potential of the tax while also containing administration and collection cost.

6 International Experiences: Resilience of Area-Based Taxes and Shifting to Simpler Beneficial Property Tax Options

Several countries have struggled with the ownership-valuation model and have moved toward simpler options linked to size, and in many cases, the alternatives are linked to local service delivery. Colombia is a successful example of property tax design and revenue generation among emerging market economies. The Bogotá example of self-valuation is of particular interest, given the success in improving revenues, although the linkages with modern tax administration are critical. Other countries have been less successful in making a transition. Mauritius moved in a related direction but, the national tax did not make the connection adequately with local benefits, and the resulting political economy constraints led to a reversal of the tax. In India, the move to a presumptive basis in some cities, such as Bengaluru, and more recent links with benefits is of interest.

6.1 *The Evolution of the English Model Toward Beneficial Property Taxes*

England has one of the longest experiences with property taxation. The use of the annual rental value in England over the years was designed to sidestep problems with valuing owner-occupancy. Earmarking the rates to finance local services, initially poor houses, and then local services established a link with benefits. The link appeared so strong to Alfred Marshall (1890) to suggest a distinction between "beneficial" and "onerous" rates. Property taxes were beneficial when used to finance services that provided corresponding benefits to taxpayers. When services were not provided, the taxes became "onerous." Also, local governments were, according again to Marshall, better suited to provide services of value because of their proximity to citizens and firms. National taxes were almost always onerous, because the national government tended and tends not to link broad-based taxes to local public goods. Since 1950 rates in England were assessed by the Inland Revenue authority, with general revaluation every five years and by requiring each property owner to inform the valuers of the market rent of his property. When property was not rented, valuation had to be based on rent of similar properties.

Residential property rates were replaced by the ill-fated "community charge" or poll tax in 1990. This was a regressive flat-rate tax paid by every adult, at a locally set rate. This tax proved very unpopular and difficult to administer due to the lack of local registries of the population.

The community charge or poll tax was, in turn, replaced by an occupancy tax in 1993. The Local Government Finance Act 1992 introduced the Council Tax, and its incidence is on occupancy—whether tenants or owners, and on owners in case the property is vacant. Only if the property is a "house in multiple occupation," does the landlord pay the council tax.

Local governments are free to set the rates whose progressivity is centrally determined by allocating each property into eight different bands (going from A to Z; see Table 1.6.) according to their value (as of 1 April

Table 1.6 England: council tax bands and rates

Band	*Value as on 1 April 1991*	*No. of properties (millions) in band in England at September 2010*	*Tax rate as a proportion of that in band D*	*Charge in local authority setting English average band D rate in 2009/10*
A	Up to £40,000	5.7	0.67	£959
B	£40,001 to £52,000	4.5	0.78	£1119
C	£52,001 to £68,000	5.0	0.89	£1279
D	£68,001 to £88,000	3.5	1.00	£1439
E	£88,001 to £120,000	2.2	1.22	£1759
F	£120,001 to £160,000	1.1	1.44	£2079
G	£160,001 to £320,000	0.8	1.67	£2398
H	More than £320,000	0.1	2.00	£2878

Source. Tax by design (Mirrlees Report), Chapter 16. *The Taxation of Land and Property*. Institute for Fiscal Studies, 2011

1991 in England and Scotland, and 1 April 2003 in Wales).[10] Most councils allow reductions for single occupancy that is levied at 75% of the total bill. This last reduction reflects, clearly, the link between cost of service and tax paid.

A problem with the English system is that while the focus is on financing local services, the system does not track variations in market valuations. Reassessment of property values, that is under the responsibility of the central tax administration, has been delayed for years—the first

[10] The rate applicable to each band has to stay in a fixed proportion to the rate applicable to band D. For low-value property this proportion is < 1, high-value property has a >1 proportion.

Newly constructed properties are also assigned a nominal 1991 value (2003 for Wales). Each local authority sets a tax rate expressed as the annual levy on a Band D property inhabited by two liable adults.

Properties were assigned a nominal 1991 (2003 for Wales) value. Each local authority sets a tax rate expressed as the annual levy on a Band D property inhabited by two adults. This is determined in relation to the cost of public services actually met directly out of Council funds.

revaluation after 1993 was planned to take place in 2007 but was postponed—and with hugely divergent spatial trends in property values it has become politically very burdensome. For instance, the cost of providing services for a property in Band H in Wimbledon (Borough of Merton) may not be very different from those north of the river Thames, say Chelsea or Knightsbridge, but the market value of the latter might be two or three times that of a similar property in Wimbledon. Although an additional "mansion tax" was proposed for the more expensive properties, it was not enacted but the stamp duty land tax (SDLT) was increased on property purchases on the higher value properties: The schedule as of 2019 is shown in Table 1.7. This "package" of property tax measures covers the costs of registration, provides revenues, and is also used to encourage equity and moderate the steep rise in property prices in central locations.

The property tax on commercial properties remains based on annual rental values. These are relatively easy to track, based on the contracts. This has the advantage of encouraging the movement of businesses to the

Table 1.7 UK property sale stamp tax on property purchases

Property or lease premium or transfer value	*SDLT rate*
Up to £125,000	Zero
The next £125,000 (the portion from £125,001 to £250,000)	2%
The next £675,000 (the portion from £250,001 to £925,000)	5%
The next £575,000 (the portion from £925,001 to £1.5 million)	10%
The remaining amount (the portion above £1.5 million)	12%

less crowded and cheaper outer areas within cities like London, or to cheaper cities in the Midlands or North-East England. This has the advantage of moving large businesses (e.g., Amazon and Federal Express) to areas that need new employment opportunities, given the loss of jobs in shipbuilding or steel. It also has the advantage of relieving the congestion pressures in London, supplementing other measures such as the fuel tax and congestion charges.

7 Other International Experiences of Property Taxes and Political Resilience of Area-Based Systems

Area-based models are popular mostly in East European transition countries, where a housing market was initiated with the fall of the “Iron Curtain,” and private ownership of housing was at an incipient state. Poland, Hungary, Bulgaria, the Czech Republic, Slovakia, and the Baltic Republics among others, use this model of recurrent property taxation (McCluskey et al. 1998; Youngman and Malme 2004). But there are several other interesting examples, as we discuss below.

7.1 Israel

Israel’s Arnona is a very productive area-based tax, and the recurrent tax that yields almost 2% of GDP (see Annex Table 1). Arnona is paid by the occupant, or owner when they differ, and is determined according to square meters, location of properties, that is, zones, type of property (apartments, individual family houses, etc.), and use (residential, industrial, retail, banks, etc.). Several exemptions based both on property and income are granted to alleviate excessive burden on poor households and properties. Despite the small number of factors used for the determination of the tax, Arnona has wide coverage.[11]

Until 1960, Arnona was based on the property’s rental value. During this period, the proportional share of public housing in the total housing stock was relatively small, and most apartments were privately owned or rented, making easy the use of the rental value of the property. In the mid-1950s–1960s, when a substantial amount of public housing was built, the Arnona tax base has been estimated based on the number of rooms for residential use, and the area of the premises used for non-residential purposes. It is interesting to note that since its introduction the definition of the tax base has changed three times.

Since 1970, the area of the property has become the dominant criterion for the tax base. The tax is calculated using the following formulation:

Property Tax = $m^2 \times t \times$ zone × use × type of property

[11] For example, the tax rate on an old house in a poor neighborhood of Tel-Aviv was, for 2020, NIS 38,87. For a villa of 140 square meters in the expensive areas of the city, the municipality charged ANAIS 1113,43. https://www.buyitinisrael.com/news/municipal-property-tax-in-israel/

Where t is tax rate expressed in New Shekels per square meter

7.2 *Bengaluru (India)*

The tax levied by the municipality of Bengaluru compares favorably with respect to the better performing value-based taxes in other Indian cities (see Table 1.2). The formula is also very simple, since it uses only a depreciation index, requiring information about age of buildings. However, area is divided into three separate components that require more articulate and frequently debatable information.

Property tax = $(G_i - I_i) \times m_i^2 \times t$ + Cess (26% of property tax)

G_i is the reference price of a square meter of property (*SMRP*) expressed in rupees × square meter.

SMRP is determined separately for tenanted area of property (X), for self-occupied area of property, Y; and for vehicle parking area (Z).

I is a depreciation index based on the age of property.

t is the rate and is set at 20%.

Cess is an additional levy, amounting to 24% of the property tax, and is earmarked for beggar support, libraries, garbage collection, and labor support.

An additional cess of 2% was introduced in 2021 for funding local transportation. The direct linkage between increases of tax and sectoral use of revenue helps the municipality to absorb the unpopularity of an expanded tax burden, partially offsetting the earlier reversal of the generalized tax increase.

7.3 *The Czech Republic*

Property taxation in the Czech Republic was reformed in 2014. Despite the government's intention to introduce a value-based model, the area-based model has been retained. The tax on residential buildings uses the following formula containing, in addition to area, location, and size of municipalities:

Tax = $m^2 \times 2CZK/m^2 + 0.75CZK/m^2 \times a_i \times b_i \times c_i$

The tax rate, two Czech krones per square meter. is nationally determined

a_i is a coefficient = 0.75 Czech krone per floor

b_i is a municipal size (population) coefficient, nationally determined and varying from 1.0 to 5.0

c_i is a location (zones) coefficient varying from 2.0 to 5.0 and is locally determined.

7.4 *Colombia*

Colombia is among the top performers concerning the property tax in Latin America, although well below the potential, and applies an area-based tax for non-registered properties. The tax is based on: (i) size; (ii) type of property (land, individual houses, and condominiums); (iii) use (residential or commercial); and (iv) quality (mix of characteristics and location) for residential buildings. The Ministry of Finance determines the values per square meter. The appropriate value is multiplied by the number of square meters to determine the tax base, to which a municipally determined tax rate is applied. Table 1.8 details the structure of the Colombian area-based tax.

7.5 *Turkey*

Turkey decided, in 2018, to replace its area-based model with a value-based one. To this purpose, the government introduced the *Valuable Real Estate Tax* (see Grover, Walacik, Buzu, Güneş, Rasković, and Yildiz, 2019

Table 1.8 Colombia: an area-based tax for non-registered properties

Use of property		*Condominiums value per M^2 of construction (Pesos)*	*Land value per M^2 of construction (Pesos)*	*Individual houses value M^2 of construction (pesos)*
Residential	1	510,326	234,893	263,510
	2	873,993	329,088	299,279
	3	1,482,091	479,325	379,167
	4	2,549,909	1,083,007	696,657
	5	3,122,877	1,271,359	971,922
	6	3,921,127	2,230,133	1,275,074
Commercial	Punctual	3,395,303	662,695	503,058
	Zonal	5,082,894	1,122,824	672,085
	Urban	7,570,009	2,336,871	802,209
	Metropolitan	11,063,242	4,334,343	1,008,798
	Financial	5,830,100	2,161,135	1,018,189

Source: Ministry of Finance of Colombia

for an illustration of the previous attempts to reform). To soften political resistance to the reform, the government granted a very high exemption threshold of 5 million TRY (about US$837,000). This shrank the number of taxpayers. Despite this provision, political resistance persisted, and the old area-based model remains in place.

7.6 Gabon

Laws passed in 1996 and 2007 introduced three different property taxes based on value, but in practice, a 1963 law is still applied that provides for a rudimentary area-based system dating back to colonial times. The absence of valuation of properties explains the survival of the old tax.

References

Ahmad E., (2015) Governance and Institutions. In Ahmad E, and Brosio, G., (eds) Handbook of Multilevel Finance. Edward Elgar, Cheltenham

Ahmad E., (2017) Political economy of tax reforms for the SDGs—improving the investment climate, addressing inequality, and stopping the cheating, Background Paper for the G24 Countries.

Ahmad E, N Stern, (1991) The theory and practice of tax reform in developing countries. Cambridge University Press.

Ahmad E, G Brosio and C Pöschl, (2015) Local property taxes and benefits in developing countries: overcoming political resistance? In: Ahmad E, and Brosio G (eds) Handbook of Multilevel Finance. Edward Elgar, Cheltenham

Ahmad E, Brosio G and Gerbrandy J., (2018) Property taxation Economic features, revenue potential and administrative issues in a development context. EU, Brussels

Ahmad, E., D. Dowling, D. Chan, S. Colenbrander and N. Godfrey, (2019), Scaling up investment for sustainable urban infrastructure: A guide to national and subnational reform, Coalition for Urban Transitions: A New Climate Economy Initiative.

Bahl R., Wallace S (2008) Reforming the Property Tax in Developing countries. A new approach. Working Paper 08-19. Andrew School of Policy Studies.

Bird R, and Rao, G., (2012) Coping with Change: The Need to Restructure Urban Governance and Finance in India. Institute on Municipal Finance and Governance.

Collier P, Glaeser E, Venables T., Manwaring P and Blake M (2018) Land and property taxes for municipal finance. International Growth Center, Oxford.

Marshall A., (1890) Principles of Economics (8th ed.), Macmillan & Co. Appendix G. Edition used: Principles of Economics. Macmillan and Co., London (8th ed. 1920), Online Library of Liberty.

McCluskey W J, Plimmer F, Connelan O., (1998) Ad valorem property tax. Issues of fairness an Equity Assessment Journal. 5 47-55.

Mirrlees Report (2011) Tax by design, Chapter 16. The Taxation of Land and Property. Institute for Fiscal Studies.

Norregaard J., (2013) Taxing Immovable Property Revenue Potential and Implementation Challenges. IMF Working Paper

OECD (2021) A Review of Local Government Finance in Israel: Reforming the Arnona System, OECD Multi-level Governance Studies, OECD Publishing, Paris, https://doi.org/10.1787/a5bc4d25-en.

Olima W., (2010) Property Taxation in Anglophone East Africa: Case Study of Mauritius 2010 Lincoln Institute of Land Policy.

Palameta B, and Macredie I., (2005) Property taxes relative to income. Statistics Canada, Perspectives, March.

Stuart Mill, J., (1848) Principles of Political Economy with some of their Applications to Social Philosophy. Book V, Chapter V Of Some Other Taxes, First Pub. Longmans, Green and Co.London

Wildasin D, and Wilson J D, (1991) Theoretical issues in local public economics. An overview, Regional Science and Urban Economics.

Youngman J, Malme J., (2004) The property tax in a new environment: Lessons from international Tyax reform effort, Lincoln land institute. Cambridge Mass.

Zodrow G., (2006) Who Pays the Property Tax? Land Lines. 18, (2): 14-19.

Zodrow G, and Mieszkowski P., (1986) Pigou, Tiebout, Property Taxation and the Underprovision of Local Public Goods. Journal of Urban Economics 19, 356-370.

CHAPTER 2

Failure and Promise of Property Taxation in Senegal

Abstract Senegal illustrates the problems with the property tax in emerging market countries. The dismal property tax collections are concentrated in the largest cities, and that too in the upscale districts in metropolitan Dakar. This leads to significant service delivery differentials in the country, with migratory pressures toward Dakar, and increasing informality in sprawling slums. Mayors do not know what is assessed, or even what is collected that goes first to the Central Treasury in Dakar, or what might finally accrue to them. This leads to a dysfunctional local government system, seriously hampering plans to create "sustainable growth hubs," including in Saint Louis, Africa's most ecologically vulnerable city but with tremendous potential. Coordinated actions on beneficial property taxes and governance reforms are recommended.

Keywords Agglomeration and growth • Colonial models of taxation • Cadastral assessment

Senegalese property tax collections are negligible, even if the revenues collected are not known with precision. In 2016, Communauté Financière Africaine Francs (CFAF) 3 bn was reported on account of budgetary central government, and the total may be in the range of CFAF 10–15 bn. IMF Staff Report for 2016 reports figures of CFAF 27 bn (0.4% of GDP) for 2014 and CFAF 31 bn for 2015.

E. Ahmad, G. Brosio, *Beneficial Property Taxation for Emerging Market Countries*, https://doi.org/10.1007/978-3-031-08612-0_2

Significant differences in property values and revenue potential obtain between the metropolitan area of Dakar and other cities in Senegal. In rural areas, there are major differences between rain-fed and irrigated areas and between forested and agricultural land that represent development challenges and point to the need for an appropriately differentiated system of property taxation. The legal framework is complicated as there were vast areas of "communal land" where traditional rights were obtained. After independence, all land was "nationalized," although this did not extinguish traditional rights and obligations in the communal lands. A hybrid system of land titles has emerged with some private property, especially in urban areas, but with a great deal of "informal" (actually illegal) settlement on state lands that is more pronounced in urban Senegal, accentuating the difficulties with rural-urban migration.

The Dakar metropolitan area houses a quarter of the population of the country. But more importantly, it generates 55% of GDP, and hosts 80% of enterprises, and 87% of local tax revenues. However, given the growing disparities in employment opportunities between Grand Dakar and the rest of the country, rural-urban migration has led to growing pressures on very stretched infrastructure in Metropolitan Dakar (World Bank 2016).

The local taxes form part of the General Tax Code, Loi 2012–31 of 31 December 2012 (see Box 2.1). A significant component includes *patentes* on services, licenses, and minimum taxes on employment or self-employment on a *forfait* basis, as well as presumptive taxes on employment and profits. Six presumptive taxes were amalgamated into the *Contribution Globale Foncière* (CGF; see *Décret* 2013–1162), to be shared between the state and local governments on a 25:75 basis (#74 of the *Code Général des Impôts*)—to be administered by the Treasury (*Direction Générale de la Comptabilité Publique et du Trésor*, or DGCP).

Despite the very extensive list of taxes, heavily influenced by the French administrative tradition, local governments have neither the power to set rates even at the margin (e.g., within a band as is often the case in unitary countries), nor are they involved in determining the base or the administration. The assessments for the property tax charges are made by the central tax administration, based on the register, and amounted to less than 0.4% of GDP in 2016, or CFAF 24.1 bn in assessed local and property taxes (data provided by Diréction Générale des Impôts Directs (DGID)). Of this, CFAF 21.2 bn was generated in the Dakar metropolitan region. As discussed below, *actual collections were typically a fraction of the assessments* for a sample of municipalities for which data was provided by the DGCP/Tresor. Indeed, neither the amounts budgeted by local governments nor the actual collections (which were a third of amounts budgeted) had any link with the assessments carried by the tax administration.

Box 2.1 Types of Local Taxes—Largely Drawing on Law 2012–31

- **Minimum Fiscal** (#270–274): a **poll tax** on the basis of individual income capacity ranging from 600 to 24,000 CFAF, with a list of exemptions
- **Representative de l'impôt du minimum fiscal** (#275–282); addressing profits of local activities but taxing **payroll**, from 900 to 36,000 CFAF
- **Contribution foncière des propriété bâties**: (#283–294); or tax on built-up properties; rate of 5% on residential and 7.5% for commercial use and factories; based on cadaster, valuation by DGID, collection by DGCP.
- **Taxe sur les ordures ménagères** (TOM); or garbage collection tax, on the basis of the cadaster, at a rate of 3.6% in the Greater Dakar region, and 3% elsewhere
- **Contribution foncière des propriété non bâties**: (#296–302), or tax on undeveloped or semi-constructed land, with a tax rate of 5% of the market value; a surtax is also permissible (#303-#307)
- **Patente**: (#320–342); presumptive tax on professions, with a fixed component by sector; and a variable component where the value varies by location and sector
- **Licenses**: for sales or consumption on location (e.g., alcoholic beverages), with rates from CFAF 35,000 to CFAF 175,000 in Dakar—lower in other areas
- **Commission de la fiscalité locale**: is responsible for the revaluation of properties (members largely nominated by the tax administration, and rural chiefs; or quarter representatives) along with the cadastral service; also can levy a surtax (#319).

Dakar's revenue base is heavily concentrated in rich municipalities (communes). A selection of assessments by the DGID in 2016 for rich and poor communes in the Dakar metropolitan areas shows the commune of NgorAlmadies (an exclusive residential and upper-end business area) is assessed at CFAF 4 billion; whereas the commune of NdiaremeLimamoulaye is assessed at around CFAF 800,000.

1 Informality, Sustainable Growth Hubs, and Property Taxes

Given the difficulties with establishing property titles, much of the expansion of population and properties have been in very poor informal settlements on the periphery of Metropolitan Dakar. This has added to congestion and unsanitary conditions and reduces the long-standing attractiveness of Metropolitan Dakar as an "international hub." Building on this favorable geographical location and potential harbor facilities is one of the factors envisaged for the longer-term growth strategy in Senegal (Kireyev and Mansur 2015).

Decentralization of the current meager property tax bases from the Ville of Dakar (the Dakar Metropolitan region) to the communes has the potential to further reduce the resources available to the poor peripheral areas of the metropolitan zone, in the absence of a proper system of equalization transfers either within Metropolitan Dakar or from the central government directly to the communes. This is likely to cause continuing congestion, and limited investments in the peripheral communes, as basic services such as paved feeder roads as well as sanitation, adequate water supplies, and garbage collection are likely to remain out of reach. Rather than adding to the attractiveness of Metropolitan Dakar as a "hub for West Africa," the growing informality can only result in increasing congestion costs and stretched local public services that would likely make it harder for firms to maintain their competitive positions.

A very significant transformation has taken place, turning Senegal from a peanut oil and raw cotton-producing country in the 1960s to a much more diversified production and export structure by the early 2000s. The authorities are correctly focusing on developing additional domestic "hubs," or growth "poles," particularly outside Metropolitan Dakar. EncouragingSmall Medium-sized Enterprises (SMEs) would be critical in enhancing both employment opportunities and realizing Senegal's production and export potential. The negative "complexity index" indicates that Senegal remains well below its potential in leveraging its natural and human resources and exports (Hausman et al. 2016). This is likely linked to the increasing congestion and informality that adds to the cost of doing business in the main cities and makes it harder to stop "cheating" and tax evasion.

Consequently, the tax reform program, especially at the local levels, must include measures linked to the sustainable growth agenda. As in other emerging market economies (see Ahmad (2021) for a description of the Mexican reforms to address informality and cheating), a rationalization of both tax policy and administration measures will be needed, involving both wide area national taxes such as the VAT that incorporates services and linked to an integrated small taxpayer regime, the income taxes and also a simplified local tax agenda. The generation of information on assets at the local level, for example, through a property tax, is closely linked with blocking the cheating in the income taxes. Local taxes are also needed to provide financing for local services to make the hubs or "poles" effective, but also in generating improved incentives for local governance and prevention of rent-seeking behavior more generally.

The continuing diversification of the location of activities and generating employment opportunities is critically dependent on the success of Senegal in creating the conditions necessary for private activity in the new "hubs." Key constraints remain the (1) ability of SMEs and households to access credit—much depends on the security of tenure to provide collateral, linked to the problems with land ownership and use; and (2) the provision of basic services by local governments to facilitate the location of private activity in the relative jurisdictions (see World Bank. 2016). Of course, both national and cross-border connectivity are critical and necessary conditions in reducing costs and in opening markets. But neither on its own is sufficient to ensure that the new "hubs" (or *Pôles de Développement*) will materialize.

2 Property Tax Collections and Potential

It is not easy to accurately estimate the revenues collected on account of property taxes in Senegal. The amounts budgeted by local governments bear little resemblance to the assessments processed by the DGID (tax administration), and the collections appear to be orthogonal to either the assessments or amounts budgeted. From the DGID figures for 2016, it appears that only around CFAF 24 bn was assessed on account of property-related taxes (including TOM). Figures from the Treasury/DGCP for the 28 most important local government municipalities (see Table 2.1) suggest that budget provisions for the FB (Foncier Bâti or property tax on built areas) and FNB (Foncier non Bâti or property tax on non built areas) were CFAF 9.7 bn and CFAF 194 m, respectively. Collections, however, were CFAF 3.4 bn for the FB (roughly a third) and CFAF 14 m for the FNB—less than a tenth of the budgeted amount. The TOM (Taxe d'ordures menagères or refuse collection tax) fared better, and the collections for the 28 municipalities were 37% of the budgeted amount. The

Table 2.1 Local tax collections for selected communes in Senegal, 2016

N° ORDRE	*COLLECTIVITES LOCALES*	*PREVISION BUDGETAIRE*				*REALISATIONS*			
		FB	*FNB*	*TOM*	*CGF*	*FB*	*FNB*	*TOM*	*CGF*
1	VILLE DE DAKAR	6,624,000,000	–	1910 000000	150,000,000	2,192,804,484		869,157,081	33,533,934
2	VILLE DE PIKINE	957,516,403		383,075,426		656,144,244		41,954,728	–
3	VILLE DE GUEDIAWAYE	175 000000	30,000,000	70 000000		53,397,945	–	38,099,641	–
4	VILLE DE RUFISQUE	646 000000	–	90 000000	–	105,171,042	–	8,711,280	
5	VILLE DE THIES	450 000000	–	30,000,000	–	49,264,966	–	13,268,584	–
6	COLOBANE	500,000	100,000	30,000	–	–	–	–	
7	MBAR	3 500,000	2 000000	–	–	–	–	–	–
8	KAOLACK	115 000000	549,600	40,454,032	7 000000	19,245,276	263,206	10,656,989	8,999,415
9	ST LOUIS	84 000000	16 000000	74 000000	8 000000	43,222,860	1,298,250	26,452,855	3,740,440
10	LOUGA	39,060,302	3 000000	25 000000	14,707,764	7,400,426	–	5,077,666	–
11	GUEOUL	1 000000	–	50,000	–	–	–	–	–
12	FOUDIOUGNE	1 000000	200,000	185,000	–	1,230,713	–	133,368	–
13	RUFISQUE EST	1,800,000	2,558,100	2 000000	–	56,250	56,250	133,935	–
14	DIOURBEL	70 000000	18 000000	21,322,436	–	10,247,531	150,000	5,948,389	–
15	DIOFFIOR	400,000	50,000	200,000	–	–	–	–	–
16	OUAKAM	25 000000	54 000000	30,000,000	–	9,994,902	423,000	1,094,096	–
17	NGOR	42,694,547	63,458,298	–		39,434,109	–	3,056,486	–
18	TIVAOUANE	3 000000	–	410,000		1,977,256		284,036	–
19	KHOMBOLE	3 000000	1 000000	5 000000	–	–	–	–	–

20	FANN-POINT E-AMITIE	80 000000	–	–	716,225	10,667,696	–	–	1,744,065
21	PIKINE NORD	–	–	–	17 185,000	–	–	–	5,108,366
22	BAKEL	1 000000	–	270,740	–	203,000	–	91,800	–
23	VELINGARA	10 000000	100,000	3 000000	–	315,600	–	714,480	–
24	RICHARD TOLL	280,188,855	50,000	3 000000	–	218,495,431	–	132,480	–
25	ZIGUINCHOR	70 000000	2 000000	25 000000	–	9,326,388	10,540,000	5,222,002	–
26	GAE	6 000000	250,000	2 500,000	–	21,450	–	113,500	–
27	KOLDA	20 000000	1 500,000	7 000000	–	384,520	2,097,811	285,960	–
28	KAFFRINE	6 000000	–	12 000000	–	221,630	–	67,400	–
	TOTAL	**9,715,660,107**	**194,815,998**	**2,734,497,634**	**197,608,989**	**3,429,327,719**	**14,828,517**	**1,030,656,756**	**53,126,226**

Source: DGCP/Tresor.
SITUATIONS D'EXECUTION DE QUELQUES COLLECTIVITES LOCALES.
FB= Impōt foncier bâti.
FNB- lùmpōt foncier non bâti.
TOM=Taxe d'enlévement des ordures ménagéres.
CGF= Contribution globale foncière.

simplified CGF procedures also performed very poorly, with only over 25% of budgeted amounts collected.

The performance of the Senegalese property taxation system is quite dismal. Assuming some correspondence between the assessed and budgeted amounts (unfortunately as we shall see for Saint Louis below, this is not always the case), we would expect that the overall collections would not have exceeded around CFAF 9–10 bn (or in the range of 0.15% of GDP). This is in line with the assumptions of collection in IMF (2017).

The IMF (2017) projected the property taxes potential of around 2% of GDP in the short-to-medium term, using a simplified base. The strengthened local revenue base is needed to put in place the financing and incentives to operationalize the new sustainable employment hubs (or *Pôles*)—with the new urban centers providing the basis for the new sustainable growth impetus. While the target is appropriate for the medium term, a more realistic target in the short-to-medium term would be around 1% of GDP.

3 The Case of Saint Louis

Strategically located Saint Louis was the capital of French West Africa, and then of French Senegal, but has decayed since the focus of activity shifted to Dakar after independence. It has several potentials in addition to the strategic location—as the focus of a fishing industry and also UNESCO World Heritage rating of the old town. However, it needs significant renovation and uplift to become a major tourist attraction. With excellent education facilities, including a top university, it has clear potential as a new employment hub.

The city faces significant sustainability challenges and was ranked as the most threatened city on the African continent by rising sea level (UN Habitat, 2012). The dredging of the river and tidal canal in 2004 was a failure and has contributed to the vulnerability of Saint Louis Island and the old city. Also, dumping of effluent and garbage into the freshwater river has poisoned the water supply and potentially jeopardized the quality of the fish farmed in the region. Much of the recent construction in and around the old city is informal, on state/communal land, and of poor quality as there are few incentives to spend resources on risky construction. Service delivery is poor, and the public finances are an indication of the dysfunctional arrangements at the local level in Senegal.

The municipal budget is a meaningless exercise. The municipal authorities have little idea about the revenue base, including central transfers, or how well funds are being utilized. Although a hard budget constraint exists in that spending is constrained by available revenues, the Municipality does not have timely information on the actual balances in their account in the Treasury. There is a quarterly report on Treasury transactions, but the process does not stop the Municipality from running arrears. In some cases, there is a deliberate gameplay with higher levels of government and State Owned Enterprises (SOE)s: the electricity company does not pay local taxes and fees, and the municipality does not pay its electricity bills. This is reminiscent of the causes of circular debt in countries like Pakistan.

The property tax circuit in Saint Louis is representative of the problems associated with local taxation in Senegal. As mentioned, a significant portion of the land is either communal or belongs to the state. Much of the construction is therefore illegal, and the inhabitants have neither a property number Numero d'identification cadastrale (cadastral identification number) (NICAD) nor an individual tax identifier number (NINEA). The municipal budget for 2016 forecasted a collection of CFAF 84 m for the built-up property tax (FB), but only 50% was collected (CFAF 43 m); and the forecast for FNB (non-built up land) was CFAF 16 m, but only 8% was collected (Table 3.3). Similarly, only 38% of the budgeted TOM was collected.

The DGID forecasted for Saint Louis a collection of FB of CFAF 126 m in 2011 to a high of CFAF 145 m in 2012, declining to CFAF 113 m in 2014. On average, CFAF 45 m has been collected in any given year, although arrears are pursued. However, a revaluation exercise led to the FB being increased to CFAF 265 m in 2016. Surprisingly, the Tresor/DGCP put the amounts to be collected in 2016 at CFAF 24.7 m—a number considerably lower than the assessments being used for previous years. The actual *Patente* collection is very erratic and there is a huge build-up of arrears that will likely never be recovered.

Part of the difficulty is the complex circuit of collections. Assessments by the local officials of DGID and the reassessments by the Commission de la fiscalité locale are passed to DGID headquarters and from there to the Treasury in Dakar. The authorizations to collect are then filtered back through regional offices to *Receveurs* (collectors) at the local level. The *Receveurs* are officials of the Treasury and have little to do with DGID officials in local tax offices, even though nominally they both fall under the same ministry. An additional difficulty is that the *Receveurs*, who do their own canvassing of properties (duplicating the work of the DGID/Tax

Committees) cannot link the NINEA or individual tax numbers to specific properties—partly because of the ownership problems. The amounts to be collected consequently bear little relation to the local budgets, and the mayors have little idea as to how much is collected.

The local *Receveurs* (DGCP/Tresor) effectively maintain taxpayer masterfiles, with manual records of what is past due and what should be paid. Unfortunately, this information is not transmitted back to the DGID. The *Receveurs* are not able to initiate or maintain audits or impose sanctions. These essential tax administration functions that should be consolidated in a reformed DGID that is organized on functional lines, including at the local level.

The *Receveurs* are able to record the arrears for registered taxpayers. However, they are not able to do anything with the information. Nor do they know the universe of unregistered properties, and the potential missing revenues. What is worrying is that even the information on revenue arrears available at the local level is lost in the cash-based accounting of the Treasury. Neither the (known) arrears on the revenue side nor those reflected on the spending side are reflected in the summary Treasury accounts.

There is no meaningful flow of information between the DGID and *Receveurs* (Tresor/DGCP) and between them and the Municipality. Consequently, there is very little scope for meaningful audit—or investigation of why the amounts demanded by DGID, or even the (lesser) amounts specified in municipal budgets, are not collected. The very sharp drop in the amounts to be collected on account of the FB/TOM during 2016 relative to previous years might have merited a call from the *Receveur* in Saint Louis to his DGID colleague down the road. Similarly, DGID discovered a tax base of CFAF 265 m because of the revaluation (more than double that in previous years) but had no idea that the collection target for the DGCP/R*eceveur* was only CFAF 26 m.

Keeping a separate body for the cadaster is also quite common, as it performs many additional legal and urban management functions. The digitalization of the land register, and issuance of land use numbers (NICAD), is an important initiative and opens the possibilities for easier ways of taxing property, as we describe in the next sections.

The transfer of taxpayer masterfiles and information on arrears from the *Receveurs* to the local DGID would permit the treasury to focus on better managing the flow of funds. As there is an ongoing reform of the Treasury Single Account, consideration should be given to creating zero-balance correspondent accounts for local governments (see Ahmad 2015) so that local *Receveurs* could better manage the flow of transactions at the local level, as well as keeping better overall track of both spending and revenue arrears.

In sum, the property tax administration is dysfunctional. While in principle it is not a bad idea to separate the setting establishment of the base of the property tax from the collection function (to avoid rent-seeking incentives), de facto this is not achieved in Senegal as the *Receveurs* tend to carry out their own evaluations of who should pay and how much, as part of the collection function. However, the amounts to be collected (set by DGID) appear to have little bearing in the work of the *Receveurs*. Thus, neither agency is responsible for the collections, or maximizing the government revenues.

4 The Sustainable Growth Agenda

Restructuring the sprawling informal settlements around Dakar, and creating new sustainable employment "hubs" around the country (*pôles de développement*) will require coordinated moves to strengthen own-sources of local finance and the establishment of a beneficial property tax to raise 1.0 of GDP in the short-to-medium term. This will involve greater local ability to set rates (within a band) as well as clarity in the determination of local functions and accountability mechanisms.

The critical issue is the choice and selection of the marginal rate at the local level, and the flow of information perhaps simplified by satellite imagery (see the Tanzanian case below) as well as greater use of blockchain. Many of the typical tax administration functions could be handled by the national tax agency.

Much will also depend on the information flows at the sub-national level, including an integrated government financial information management system that uses a standard GFSM 2014-compliant Chart of Accounts. This will permit more accurate and speedy information for the mayors as well as the local Treasury officials, so that there is enhanced local accountability including for arrears and liabilities and more efficient incentives for better revenue generation and spending.

References

Ahmad E., (2015) Governance and Institutions. In Ahmad E, and Brosio, G., (eds) Handbook of Multilevel Finance. Edward Elgar, Cheltenham

Ahmad, E., (2021) "National and Subnational Tax Reforms to Address Informality," in C. Deléchat and L. Medina, eds., The Global Informal Workforce, IMF, Washington DC, 2021.

Hausman R. et al. (2016) Atlas of Economic Complexity, Harvard-MIT Complexity Project.

IMF (2017) Senegal: Staff Report for the 2016 Consultation, CR 17/02, p. 36.

Kireyev A, and Mansur A., (2015) Making Senegal a Hub for West Africa, IMF.

World Bank (2016). Revue de l'urbanisation: Villes Émergents pour un Sénégal Emergent.

CHAPTER 3

Challenges of Property Taxation in Tanzania

Abstract Corruption has been a big problem in Tanzania, which operated the colonial tax administrator model, with a complex arrangement requiring qualified surveyors to verify property values in a country with very few qualified surveyors. Attempts were made to simplify and centralize the tax base on an area-related basis, with pilots in Ilala and Mwanza, and the of use satellite imagery in the latter supplemented by low-tech verification. Inadequate software created problems with digital registration. There was political resistance to centralization of the revenue collections, given that automatic flow of funds to municipal accounts is not assured—leading to a reversal of the centralization. Experimentation with new technologies, such as the blockchain, could resolve the problems with information flows on both the revenue collections, potentially limiting rent-seeking opportunities, and flow of funds back to municipal accounts with a simplification of financial management procedures.

Keywords Central versus local administration • Land use models • Capturing information with digital techniques

Corruption has been pervasive in Tanzania, affecting all levels of government and administration, and the late President Magufuli since his election in 2015 made fighting corruption and the implementation of the rule

E. Ahmad, G. Brosio, *Beneficial Property Taxation for Emerging Market Countries*, https://doi.org/10.1007/978-3-031-08612-0_3

of law two of the main axes of his administration. According to the 2016 Corruption Perceptions Index by Transparency International, Tanzania was ranked 116th out of 175 countries (with 175 being the most corrupt). Tax officials were perceived as the most corrupt (see information provided by *Afrobarometer*).

The yield of the property tax in Tanzania is almost negligible—reflecting evasion or avoidance by the rich taxpayers, as well as political resistance. As a response to inefficiency and corruption, the Magufuli government pursued centralization of the administration and collection of the tax through the Tanzania Revenue Authority (TRA). However, centralization was viewed by the political opposition as an instrument to curb its power, since most of the big cities, including Dar es Salaam, where much of the property tax base is concentrated, were run by the opposition. To some extent this reflects the lack of clarity and relevant details with which centralization was introduced, as we will see later. In principle, with the local rate setting, and allocation of revenues remaining at the local level, the tax would be effectively local—with potentially significantly greater revenues, even if administration is centralized. The reversal of the administration centralization without addressing the key lacunae will likely have a marginal impact.

A major difficulty in Tanzania is the separation of property taxation into the rent fees and the property tax, administered by different agencies with no communication between them. Also, obstacles lie in the definition of the base of the property tax covering only the value of buildings and improvements. The assessment is complex and requires qualified surveyors that are in short supply.

Also, as in Senegal, the property tax in Tanzania covers a small percentage of properties, even in the urban areas. Most land is "Village land" which comes under the management of villages, which can grant use rights. The land tenure system in Tanzania is subject to intense conflict between traditional conventions, revived in the framework of Nyerere's *ujamaa vision,* and the modern economy. The rent fees are not applicable on village land, while the property tax can be levied in principle on modern properties built on this land.

Tanzania is a rapidly urbanizing country, although the overall urbanization rate remains low (29.1% in 2012; see Wenban Smith 2014). The population of the capital city, Dar es Salaam of over 4 million, grew 6.5% in the decade between the last two censuses, and its growth rate exceeds the national rate. The size of the second, third, and fourth largest cities, Mwanza, Dodoma and Arusha, respectively, lags largely behind Dar es

Salaam, with populations of less than half a million people. Also, the three cities are located in the northern part of the country and still reflect the pre-independence unbalanced urbanization path.

The growth of cities, especially Dar es Salaam, is driven by the construction and service sectors. Investment in real estate is massive, absorbing huge amounts of capital. However, the increase in the value of the immovable property stock has not been commensurately reflected in the property tax collections. Although there are no recent estimates about the size of the informal sector (at the end of last century two-thirds of the labor market was estimated to be informal), informal activities are still pervasive, being fueled by excessive regulation and insufficient provision of services in both the urban areas (particularly transportation and health) and the rural areas (the failure of the village development program).

The extent of informality is a huge constraint for the ownership-valuation tax administration model. According to the World Bank (2002), 70% of Dar es Salaam's population lives in poor, unplanned settlements. Residents are usually too poor to pay for services or infrastructure and the authorities are too resource-constrained to maintain these. Thus, health and environmental conditions are generally extremely poor (Collier and Jones 2016). Access to clean water and sanitation are major problems for Dar es Salaam's poor, and contribute to widespread illness, including cholera, malaria, lymphatic filariasis, and diarrhea, particularly during flood episodes, which could be more severe or frequent in future due to climate change. Poor access to public health services for the poor and informal groups has likely also played a role in the current pandemic in Tanzania, as in much of Africa. Congestion and pollution are also extremely high, especially in Dar es Salaam. The relatively small size of the other main cities in Tanzania is reflected in lower, although growing, congestion and pollution.

Mainland Tanzania is a unitary state with 37 urban governments (19 Municipalities, 15 Town Councils, and 4 Cities). Rural areas are governed by 133 Rural District Councils consisting of 2918 registered villages and 64,691 Vitongoji (hamlets).[1] Zanzibar is constitutionally an "integral part

[1] The main legislation includes: The Local Government (District Authorities) Act 19823b and the Local Government (Urban Authorities) Act 19823c provide for the establishment of rural and urban LGAs as district township authorities (villages that are assuming an urban character) and village authorities. The Acts were amended in 1999 by the Local Government Laws (Miscellaneous Amendments) Act (No. 9) 1999. Other important legislations include the Local Government Finances Act 1982, the Urban Authorities (Rating) Act 1983 amended in 2005 to grant rural districts the power to levy the property tax, the Local Authorities Elections Act 1979, and the Regional Administration Act 1997.

of Tanzania" and has its own President and a House of Representatives responsible for legislation on all domestic matters and, in practice, external trade.[2] It has also its own system of local government.

1 Property Taxation in Tanzania: General Features

Officially, only the property tax instrument is recognized. But an additional instrument is the land rent fee, that is a tax on general land, based on size and use. Despite the availability of two tax instruments, property taxation contributes only roughly 0.16% of the GDP.[3] This is well below the potential predicted by Bahl and Wallace for emerging market countries, and well below the levels achieved in the South African case (see Chap. 1).

Property taxes and land rent form a negligible part of total local own-source revenues—with the produce cess, service and hotel levies, licenses, and fees making up the rest (Table 3.1).

The property tax is levied on the improved value of land, that is, on buildings, while land rent fees are based on non-developed land. There is also no overlapping of assignments. The property tax is assigned to be collected by local governments. The Ministry of Lands, Housing and Human Settlements Development is responsible for collecting the land rent fees. In principle, the value of buildings and improvements must be deducted from the total value of property to determine the pure land value on which to set the rent fees (30% shared with local governments), while the value of undeveloped land must be deducted from improved land to determine improvements to levy the property tax. The Minister of Land has resolved the problem by simplifying the assessment of the tax base by use of a parametric method (see below). Local Councils and presently also TRA faced the complications of the choice of built-up land as the tax base. There is no sharing of tasks and information between the Ministry of Lands, Housing and Human Settlements Development and the local authorities, and this duplication is costly and inefficient.

[2] http:// www.constituteproject.org

[3] Land fees collected in fiscal year 2015–6 amounted to 74 billion Tsh, corresponding to 0.008 of GDP. In Table 4.4 collections of property tax are on average about three times the land fees, which in turn is 30% of total national collections. The equality between property tax and land fees revenue brings the total to 0.16% of the GDP.

Table 3.1 Average local revenue sources for the period of 2007/8–2011/2 in million Tsh

Name of the zone	*Property taxes*	*Land rent*	*Produce cess*	*Service levy*	*Hotel levy*	*Permit/ licenses*	*Fees*	*Other*	*Total*	*% of the total*
Central Zone	3244	589	688	5425	466	2825	2883	5301	21,423	40
Lake Zone	194	125	3654	872	310	618	1326	1097	8197	15
Northern Zone	940	698	212	1668	150	1486	2387	1362	8903	17
Southern Highlands	471	97	1992	641	134	918	2227	4365	10,846	20
Southern Zone	148	188	1561	239	103	123	245	1558	4165	8
Total	**4997**	**1698**	**8107**	**846**	**1163**	**5970**	**9068**	**13,685**	**53,534**	**100**

Source Council Financial Reports (CFR)—2007/8–2011/2

There is no official statistical information collected at the national level on property tax revenue and other characteristics of the levies. Central reports have to rely on information collected at the local level. There is a lack of comparability, and the quality of information suffers, showing weakness in the system of public financial management (PFM) in Tanzania. This leads to distrust and conflict among governments, and lack of accountability, as in Senegal.

1.1 Land Tenure Regime

Land in mainland Tanzania falls into three types: (1) village land; (2) reserved land; and (3) general land. This is shown in Fig. 3.1. Village land covers approximately 70% of mainland Tanzania and accommodates about 30 million people in 2012. Registered villages can assign land to three categories of use: (a) communal village land; (b) individual, families land; and (c) reserved land. However, in practice only a minority of villages are registered and empowered to define uses. Land assigned to families and individuals can be transferred only within the village.

As the country grows, the granting of occupancy rights to activities, such as mining, timber production, large-scale farming, tourism, and conservation erodes the area of village land. This creates frequent opposition, and also harsh conflict with the local population and village authorities,

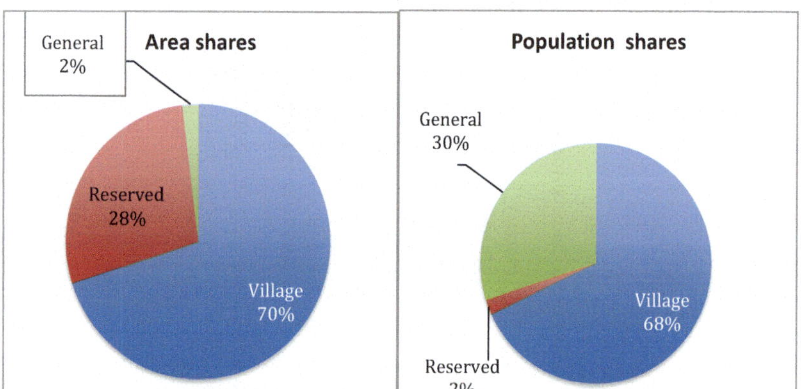

Fig. 3.1 Land tenure in Tanzania

particularly on projects that potentially endanger the environment. An increasing number of people are now living in modern dwellings that should become liable to property taxation. After the granting of occupancy rights by the Ministry of Lands, Housing and Human Settlements Development, village land becomes general land and is removed from the jurisdiction of village authorities, becoming liable to property tax under the responsibility of Rural Districts. These districts, however, have never levied the tax in the past (Center for International Development and Environment World Resources Institute, 1995)[4] and illustrate the acute political economy constraints.

Land rent fees are also not levied on plots in village land that have received occupancy rights, partly because of legal reasons, since the villages are responsible for its use, and partly to avoid conflict. An obvious action for the Ministry of Lands would be to levy the rent fee and return the proceeds to the villages.

Reserved land is set aside for natural parks, conservation areas, forest, and game reserves. It amounts to 28.5% of mainland Tanzania and in principle cannot be occupied. Despite the legal ban, it is estimated that 300,000–1,000,000 people live on reserved land, mainly pastoralists, displaced people, or even small-scale informal tourist ventures.

General land is neither village land nor reserved land. It covers only 2% of the national mainland areas and accommodated about 13 million people in 2012. Most of the general land is situated in the urban areas, with a small portion of it located in the rural areas.

1.2 Property Tax

The administration and collection process starts with the definition by local councils of the "rateable area" with built-up plots. Councils then should survey the plots and assess their value (this is also done separately and without any communication by Ministry of Lands). The process requires qualified surveyors, and only 130 were available nation-wide in 2017. As a result, despite frequent, donor-supported, surveying campaigns, the number of surveyed plots remains very small.

Surveyors assess property values based on building costs, with deductions for depreciation of buildings. Values can be well below market

[4] Districts are local government authorities and were permitted after the 2005 amendment of the Urban Authorities (Rating) Act to levy the property tax.

values, and the comparison is not immediate since market value includes necessarily the value of pure land. Taxpayers can object to their assessed value, in which case the dispute is brought to The District Land and Housing Tribunal. The whole process takes at least a year.

The tax due is calculated by applying the locally determined tax rates (up to a maximum of 0.15% for residential property, and up to 0.2% for commercial/industrial properties) to the assessed value. A typical area-based tax applies to the (majority) non-surveyed plots. The tax due is derived from multiplication by the number of square meters of a unit tax determined for different categories of use and according to the location.

Both surveyed and non-surveyed plots are recorded manually, in most cases, on paper registers. In general, the level of effort exerted by Councils has been low, generating minimal collections and prompting moves by the central government to centralize the whole administration process.

Between fiscal years 2007–8 and 2011–2 the government assigned to the TRA the administration and collection of property tax for a group of eight municipalities, including the three biggest ones in the Dar es Salaam area. However, during the pilot experiment period the TRA performance was quite weak, as shown in Fig. 3.2 referring to the three biggest municipalities in Dar es Salaam.[5] It appears that the TRA was attempting to maintain the old processes and procedures for property tax collections. Basically, there was non-cooperation, if not outright hostility, from the municipalities in the provision of information, and of seconded personnel to TRA. Also, the latter had realistically limited incentives to invest considerably in the administration of an unpopular tax with very small revenue.

After the pilot period and the return of administration to municipalities, collections increased sharply. In Kinondoni the increase was more than threefold (see Fig. 3.2). This may be that TRA operated during the pilot experiment with low efficiency and sub-optimal effort. Also, Councils had traditionally neglected the administration of property tax to such a large extent that even a modest increase of effort was able to produce substantial results. In Kinondoni, the payment of property tax was facilitated with the introduction of mobile phone-based money payment systems like M-Pesa and the electronic payment system Max Malipo. Also, the municipality started to use Mtaa (sub-wards) leaders to notify property owners.

[5] It must be noted that the impact on collection of centralization is observable with a lag of one year. This explains why in Fig. 3.4. the period of reference is 2008/9–2013/4.

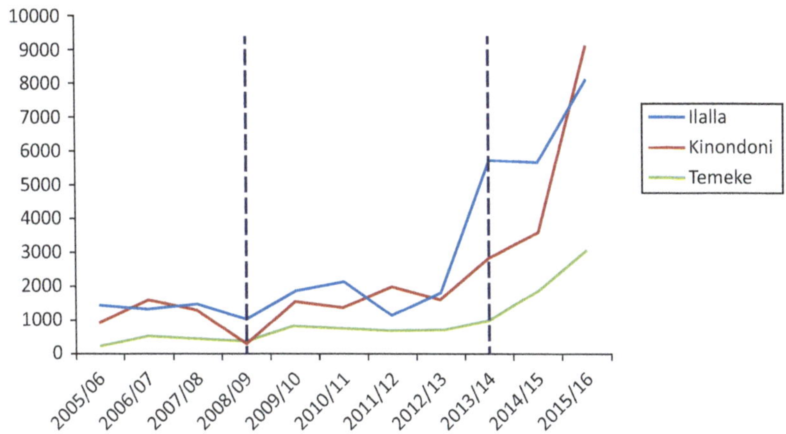

Fig. 3.2 Municipal property tax in Dar es Salam before, during, and after the experimental assignment of administration to TRA. Note: This reflects the collections of property tax in the three largest municipalities of Dar es Salaam, before, during, and after the experimental assignment of administration to the TRA. Source Fjeldstad and Katera 2017

The attempt was to transform the tax collection mechanisms to reduce corruption.

In 2016–7, the administration and collection reverted again to the TRA. According to the Budget Speech 2016/7, the decision was based on: "LGAs own sources were below the target due to inefficient revenue collection systems and low property tax collection compared to the available potential." However, the law did not specify details for the handing over of responsibilities, leaving in the vacuum, the management and even more importantly the allocation of the collections.[6] Presently, collected funds are transferred from the commercial banks to a TRA account at the central bank, to which local councils have no access.

[6] The budget mandates, without further detail, the Tanzania Revenue Authority, to undertake the responsibility.

(i) To estimate tax and make valuation of the properties; (ii) to collect property tax under its laid down procedures by using the relevant tax laws; (iii) to institute proper procedures for remittance of property tax collected by Tanzania Revenue Authority in the respective local governments; (iv) to set the procedure for dispute resolution arising from collection of property tax by using prevailing tax laws; and (v) to review property tax exemptions to ensure that more properties are brought into the tax structure.

A centralization of revenue collection also must be accompanied by Public Financial Management (PFM) reforms. An example is the creation of correspondent accounts for local governments within the Treasury Single Account. Given the payments and clearing mechanisms, these could feed local zero-balance accounts, on which local governments might be able to draw. This is to ensure rapid access to own-source revenues. Although the links between local tax reforms and the PFM system are important and were also highlighted for Senegal, this issue is seldom linked in either government policies or donor advice.

Visits to the TRA branches operating municipalities of Ilala and Mwanza testify that the approach to administration varies substantially between the two cases as shown below.

Satellite imagery and other new IT procedures for assessment of value and payment were piloted in a small group of municipalities, including Arusha and Mwanza, since 2013. The project, Tanzania Strategic Cities Project, has been sponsored by Danida and the World Bank. We examine the Mwanza experiment below.

1.3 Land Rent Fees

Land rent fees are levied only on general land, amounting to only 2% of mainland Tanzania, and are managed and collected by the Ministry for Lands, Urban Settlements Development. The legal basis is the granting of the right of occupancy to specific individuals or firms, who then become liable to the fee.[7]

The amount of rent fee is determined by multiplying the unit tax per square meter which is determined according to the use of land by the number of square meters. According to the Ministry, 1,200,000 plots are recorded and collections amount to 74 billion Tsh in 2015–6 corresponding to a mere 0.08% of the GDP, as mentioned above.

According to the law, the Ministry must assign 30% of the collections to local councils as per the derivation principle. The allocation practice has

[7] Obtaining an occupancy right is the first step towards recognition of the property title, officially labeled as the "Occupancy certificate." The certificate is granted upon request after the completion of the survey of the plot by the Ministry and validated by the Validation Commission. Occupancy certificates represent a leasehold title with durations of 33, 66, or 99 years. This is a transferable title and, as a consequence, can be mortgaged. Informal settlers without the occupancy right are not liable to the rent tax. Occupancy rights are recorded in a register managed by the Ministry.

corresponded to the legal requirement, as confirmed by Table 3.4, that includes the rent fees. Since fiscal year 2016–7 the allocation among Councils will be decided autonomously by the Ministry on the basis, it appears, of their cooperation on land tenure issues. No legal source on the change was mentioned to the mission. The process of devolution seems to become completely obfuscated.

1.4 Own-Taxes and Intergovernmental Transfers

In 2012/3, Local Government Authority (LGA) tax revenues represented 8% of total revenues of TZS 3.3 trillion, or approximately TZS 73,000 per capita on average.[8] Recurrent transfers accounted for 70% of LGA revenues in 2012/3. Development transfers with a share of approximately 21% of LGA revenues in the same year complete the local revenue sources.

There are three main types of transfers: recurrent block (i.e., grants for specific areas of activity composed of specific allocations for wages and salaries and others for operating expenses), subventions (including specific funds), and capital development grants. While subventions and donor-specific funds (called basket funds) form part of the development budget, in practice they fund expenditures that are recurrent in nature. Capital development grants fund local government infrastructure and include the discretionary Local Government Capital Development Grant (LGCDG) and sector development grants.

The government has tried over the years to improve the efficiency and transparency of the transfer allocation using "objective" formulas, based on various determinants of need (see Table 3.2). Their impact is, however, impossible to ascertain given the fragmentation of transfers, unrelated to the formulae. The obfuscation prevailing in practice offsets any efficiency aspects of the formulae. Moreover, and more importantly, the arbitrary nature of the transfers negates the potential accountability potential of own-source revenues. There is also no incentive to use the own-source revenues, since the formulas for allocation do not include indicators of tax effort or of tax capacity, resulting in the poor revenue effort and low levels of collections. In this context, the centralization of administration to TRA makes sense, although steps need to be taken not to override local autonomy. For local own-source control of a tax, it would be sufficient for local governments to set the rates at the margin (e.g., within a band determined

[8] This information is taken from *Local Government Authority (LGA)* 2014.

Table 3.2 Overview of formulae for grants to LGAs sector block grant (recurrent)

	Allocation formulae
Primary education	Number of school-aged children: 100% (earmarked amount for special schools)
Health	Population: 70%; number of poor residents: 10%; district medical vehicle route: 10%; under-five mortality: 10%
Agriculture extension	Number of villages: 80%; rural population: 10%; rainfall index: 10%
Water	Equal shares: 10%; number of unserved rural residents: 90%
Local roads	Road network length: 75%; land area (capped): 15%; number of poor residents: 10%
General purpose grant	Fixed lump sum: 10%; total number of villages: 10%; total population: 50%; total number of rural residents: 30%
Development grants	
Local Government Development Grant (LGDG)	Total population: 70%; number of poor residents: 20%; land area (capped): 10%
Sector windows of the LGDG	Same as for the respective recurrent sector grants

Source: See footnote 7

by a national legislature in a unitary state). It is equally important for the national administration to be at arm's length and not subject to local rent-seeking disincentives (see Ahmad 2015).

2 City of Ilala

Ilala provides an interesting case to study the reassignment of the administration of the tax to TRA because of the size of its tax base due to its location in central Dar es Salaam. A new Director, who was a former surveyor in the municipality, was appointed and in turn hired new staff with temporary contracts. Taxpayers were identified by using previous registers and/or by using a local network of sub-ward "street" agents (showing central-local cooperation) in the field.

Taxpayers self-declare by detailing the physical characteristics of their dwelling, such as the size and the materials used for each room and annexes, the age, and the location. The form used is very lengthy and detailed, hence difficult to fill, leading to frequent mistakes by taxpayers, and needs checking. In Ilala the problem was temporarily solved by asking the taxpayer to make a self-declaration of the value of his property. The

Table 3.3 Actual and targeted collections of property tax before and after centralization of administration and collection. (Millions Tsh)

	Mwanza	*Ilemela*	*Geita*	*Ilala*
Actual collections 2015–6	1660	1920	145	8000
Target collections 2016–7	2225	2500	160	12,500

Source: Information provided by officials

declared value was used for the determination of the tax due for the first year (2016–7) for those taxpayers for whom no assessed value has been made available by the local Council.

From 2017 the zonal TRA intended to proceed to valuation of properties making use of the information provided in the forms. This implied making the determination of the value in accordance with the old approach, based on building cost minus depreciation. This required the services of qualified surveyors. The lengthy process combined with the lack of surveyors kept the number of assessed properties quite low. According to the information provided by the tax administration officials, the number of properties in Ilala was about 350,000, but only 155,000 were in the records.

TRA tried to meet the rather ambitious collections target set up by the Municipal Council before the centralization. Target collections are shown in Table 3.3. However, the continued use of sub-ward agents to reach taxpayers could have perpetuated rent-seeking, and inability to meet targets.

Collections go from commercial banks to the central bank account for reallocation to the city that has no immediate access to the accounts collected. This is an incomplete PFM circuit, as pointed out earlier, and will likely lead to resistance on the part of local governments—this is in addition to the lower possibilities of rent-seeking.

3 Experiments in Mwanza

Mwanza provides a case study of the use of satellite imagery to determine property locations (*Tanzania Strategic Cities Project*), supplemented by low-tech verification. Locally trained students distributed forms to residents to fill in the characteristics of buildings. The information collected and checked was used for determining an area-based tax. This could also have served to check the value of properties on which the Council, before (or after) centralization, levied the property tax. However, this is not sufficient for valuation that requires the work of a surveyor. In Mwanza, only the local TRA director, who as in Ilala was a former surveyor in the municipality, had this qualification. At best, he was able to conduct personally around 2000 valuations per year. This implied that TRA was forced to rely on previous valuations, together with a relatively few updates.

Twenty years would have been needed, with existing staff, to check the 40,000 properties out of 150,000 properties in the three cities of Mwanza, Ilelena, and Geita, subject to authority of the zonal TRA. With a staff of five surveyors, the time to complete the reassessment could have been reduced to five years. This again confirms the bottlenecks represented by the valuation-based system for determining the tax base. Sidestepping the valuation requirements with an area-based tax linked to service delivery would considerably simplify the procedures to facilitate greater compliance.

The Mwanza experiment used satellite imagery for the property register: zones were specified, and buildings in these zones were identified by drawing their outlines on the map. Each building was given a number and a code. Often, this was the first time these buildings were identified, and this method effectively gave them an address. Locally trained students then visited these buildings and collected detailed information about these buildings and their occupants, using a form like that used in Ilala, and took pictures with their mobile phones. This information was then entered into the database. The result is "Geodatabase" of properties. In addition to being a relatively simple collection of essential data, it also comes with some data analysis functionality: the map can be rendered in different ways by coloring buildings on the basis of use, value, tax liabilities, and so on.

Tax due for the area-based rate was then determined on the basis of the collected information, and bills are distributed via a local network of subward agents. Tax payments could also be made at commercial banks.

The software used the Local Government Revenue Collection Information System (LGRCIS), developed by Dayone, a systems integration company from Dar es Salaam, as part of the Tanzania Strategic Cities Project. The software can be improved in different ways. For example, all flows of information were not digitized. Maps were printed out and given to local surveyors, who then had to find the building, collect information on paper, and physically bring these forms to a central office, where the data were then entered into the computer system. It would have been much more efficient if surveyors had electronic access to the map while in the field, and directly entered the information on an application n a mobile phone. A GPS-enabled mobile phone could eliminate the error of misidentifying buildings.

In the areas around Mwanza, internet connectivity was not sufficiently available, but distributed database technology could operate without internet connections. The blockchain is an example, but more consolidated technology exists as well and is a common component of modern mobile applications, such as Google Maps. Such technology can also be used as a workaround for the lack of local Information and Communication Technologies (ICT) infrastructure, and the present slow connectivity and breakdowns of the centralized system.

The system was not integrated with the Government's Property Rent Management System (PRMS): the data in the two software systems were not linked. This means that part of the administration had to be done twice by the local administration; it also implied that the TRA itself did not have access to the data in the LGRCIS system, and that data from the PRMS system (such as data on payments) were not available in the LGRCIS.

Companies such as Google and Facebook publish the source code of parts of their software stack under an open-source license so that it can be used and easily improved upon by others. The LGRCIS source code is proprietary, and this holds back further development or even basic auditing and improvements by technically competent users. There is no good reason why software that is developed with public funding for the public sector should not be a public resource itself.

TRA performance had not been satisfactory enough and in February 2021 the central government decided to return the administration of the property tax to local governments. During fiscal year 2019/20, 561.12 bn was collected, representing approximately 75% of the target. Clearly the decision to again decentralize administration was influenced by lack of incentives and poor coordination across different taxes.

4 Conclusions

Administration, whether local or central, facilitated by high-tech satellite imagery and direct payments through banks or smartphones, supported by low-tech verification, should help consolidate the system, and prevent corruption. But the political economy of linking the taxes to local benefits is essential in aligning incentives, ensuring greater local accountability. The important issue is the setting of rates at the margin and maintaining an arm's length administration, whether local or central.

As in Senegal, it is important to ensure full exchange of information between the tax collectors, the Central Treasury, and the local governments. Blockchain presents an opportunity to simplify and integrate the revenue and Treasury circuits, and to prevent leakages and rent-seeking.

References

Ahmad E., (2015) Governance and Institutions. In Ahmad E, and Brosio, G., (eds) Handbook of Multilevel Finance. Edward Elgar, Cheltenham

Collier P, and Jones P., (2016) Transforming Dar es Salaam into a City that Works, https://urbanisation.econ.ox.ac.uk/materials/papers/73/collierjonesdaressalaam.p

Fjeldstad O-H, and Katera L., (2017) Taxing the urban boom in Tanzania: central-local government relations in property tax collection in Tanzania REPOA's 22nd Annual Research Workshop.

Wenban Smith H B., (2014) Population growth, internal migration and urbanization in Tanzania, 1967-2012. A Census based regional analysis. International Growth Center, Working Paper.

World Bank (2002) Dar Es Salaam Case Study Overview Climate Change, Disaster Risk And The Urban Poor: Cities Building Resilience For A Changing World,

CHAPTER 4

Financing Sustainable Local Spending and Infrastructure in China

Abstract China lacks a recurrent tax on residential properties, as ownership-valuation experiments in Shanghai and Chongqing failed to generate revenues. Instead, local governments have increasingly relied on land sales accruing to off-budget investment corporations and partnerships with property developers. The land sale model has resulted in urban sprawl and unsustainable migrations to the coastal mega metropolises, loss of prime agricultural and wetlands, but also increasing liabilities and rent-seeking opportunities. Simulations of the beneficial property tax model show that adequate revenues (1.5–2% of the GDP) can be raised quickly to replace land sales, be progressive, and anchor basic services and a more effective local government bond system. However, a within-province equalization system is likely to be needed in conjunction. A series of pilots were initiated by the State Council in 2021, as an effective local property tax is critical in ensuring adaptation in Chinese cities to meet distributional and environmental targets in the medium term.

Keywords Diffusing spatial growth • Beneficial-tax simulation • Local tax autonomy

This chapter is based on Ahmad, E., M. Niu, L. Wang, and M. Wang, 2021

E. Ahmad, G. Brosio, *Beneficial Property Taxation for Emerging Market Countries*, https://doi.org/10.1007/978-3-031-08612-0_4

An effective property tax is essential to further the agenda of high-quality growth in Chinese cities, and to achieve the rebalancing to address the recovery from the pandemic, including the shift from coastal metropolitan areas to clean, compact cities (CCCs) in the interior, and effective provision of basic services. The tax should generate appropriate incentives for local governments to ensure better public services, including health care, and unlock sustainable access to financing for public investments. It also provides an alternative to land sales that generates urban sprawl, and off-budget financing arrangements that lead to rent-seeking behavior and debt spirals. US-type property tax models have not worked well in experiments in Shanghai and Chongqing (or any emerging market economy for that matter), and Chinese local governments remain dependent on the main instrument under their control—land sales revenues to supplement shared revenues and central transfers in periods of increasing budgetary pressure.

China's fiscal reforms since 1993/4 have focused on creating modern wide-area tax instruments at the national level, such as the VAT and broad-based income and corporate taxation, as well as administration, in keeping with international best practice. These taxes were designed, initially, to generate revenues, but increasingly to create a unified economic space, reduce the cost of doing business, and address concerns about inequality and environmental degradation (Ahmad et al. 2013; Ahmad 2018). The integration of the local business tax on services with the national VAT in 2015 was a continuation of this process. Bringing the full value chain under the VAT also provided information on transactions that provide information to reduce leakages in the income taxes (as was the case in Mexico in 2013—see Ahmad 2021).

The creation and progressive strengthening of a modern national tax agency, the State Taxation Administration (STA), permits China to manage information-based modern tax systems. This has also led to an inexorable "recentralization of the revenue system" (Ahmad et al. 2002). However, spending remains largely decentralized (or rather deconcentrated), including implementation of most local infrastructure and public service delivery, including for basic education and preventive health care. This has led to a significant "vertical imbalance" that is mainly addressed through shared revenues and transfers. These shared revenues and transfers, even if untied, cannot be a satisfactory basis for accessing credit and a local bond system (Ahmad 2021). Thus, local jurisdictions cannot vary the rate on a revenue base to meet additional debt servicing liabilities, as the shared revenues are designed to meet required spending on basic services. Indeed, as the central government reduces national tax rates for macro-economic stabilization purposes, there is a corresponding squeeze on the local governments' revenue shares meant to cover essential spending, as well as additional debt servicing requirements. This has put a telescoping pressure on sub-national level governments, which increases at the lowest levels that are also responsible for much of the basic spending needs (Xiao 2018).

Local governments in China have consequently relied heavily on taxation of property transactions, especially land sales, to finance infrastructure extrapolating from the Hong Kong model of "land value capture." This is based on selling land to developers and placing the assets and liabilities in off-budget Local Government Financing Vehicles (LGFVs). Although local governments were not permitted to borrow directly prior to 2015, the LGFVs could do so in the expectation that the proceeds would be directed to investment in a crude version of a "golden rule."

With incomplete information generated at the county level on the buildup of liabilities and the absence of own-source revenues, local governments have incentives to rely on increasing debt. This leads to soft-budget constraints and possibilities of a debt spiral, and together with poor service delivery, limits the possibility of relying on new county-level cities to "rebalance" the economy. The simulations in Sections 2 and 3 of this chapter are based on Ahmad, Niu, Wang and Wang, 2021.

1 Chinese Practices for Taxing Property

Since the centralization of tax policy and administration initiated in 1993/4, land sales provide the bulk of local revenues generating well over 1.5% of the GDP. The problems with the land sales option have been clear for some time (see Wang et al. 2018), but so far, the absence of an appropriate recurrent taxation option has proved to be a significant constraint. This also weakens and compromises the system of sustainable access to private financing and management of local risks.

Property taxation in China is exclusively on non-recurrent taxation of property transactions, and on business properties. The details are outlined below, and there are many useful features that can be easily extrapolated to other taxes—for example, central legislation with bands, allowing lower levels to set rates to suit their circumstances and needs. This is important to anchor access to credit, but property sales are too volatile to provide an adequate base.

With the disappointing pilots of variants of the ownership-valuation property tax model in Shanghai and Chongqing, there is effectively no recurrent taxation of residential properties in China. Suggestions to implement a US-style property tax, while providing household-specific exemptions at the local level (Zhi Liu 2018), could lead to corruption and rent-seeking activities.

Replacement of the Hong Kong-style land sales/land value capture model has become urgent with the collapse of some of the biggest private developers that has been in place for almost a quarter of a century. This could lead to a loss of 1.5–2% of the GDP, or a significant proportion of local revenues, so a replacement becomes urgent, and the State Council at the end of 2021 authorized a series of pilots, envisaged in the 14th Five-Year Plan. Most of the other instruments currently in use relate to taxing land transactions and are by and large appropriate. However, they generate limited revenue streams, but the design also suggests extensions that can be used for recurrent property taxation.

A recurrent property tax on households in China should not only provide an alternative to land sales in financing basic spending, but also lay the basis for access to financing on a sustainable basis, including for the system of municipal bonds, Public Private Partnerships (PPPs), and financing the generation of long-term liabilities for sustainable growth.

1.1 The Land Sales/Value Capture Model

Local financing from land sales expanded rapidly after the 1993/4 reforms with the progressive centralization of the tax assignments and revenue administration. As local governments were allowed to keep 100% of land conveyance charges that were typically placed in LGFVs that were permitted to borrow, whereas local governments were unable to borrow directly prior to 2015. Land sales provided the bulk of property-related revenues for local governments (over 1.5% of the GDP—see Salm 2017). This also formed the basis for leveraged access to credit, as a major, albeit volatile, source for financing infrastructure, especially in the main metropolitan areas along the East Coast in China. This financing played a major role in financing the expansion of employment "hubs" geared largely to export markets. The "land value capture" was facilitated by a much lower compensation provided to farmers and contributed to the sharp rise in inequality in China.

Wen, Wu, and Ye (2018) criticized the land sale financing arrangement, arguing that "the rampant negotiation-based land transactions gave rise to various problems, including corruption, inefficient use of land, land hoarding, the engulfment of prime agricultural land."

This process also led to a huge increase in ecological vulnerability. due to loss of prime agricultural and wetlands. The main ecological problems with land sales have been widely documented (see the survey in Wang et al. 2018) and include:

- *Urban sprawl* especially in the coastal mega-metropolises, with attended pressure on traffic and infrastructure leading to congestion and pollution; and a consequence is that
- The *loss of wetlands* makes the main river deltas extremely prone to flooding, and natural disasters; and
- The *loss of prime agricultural land* makes the country more vulnerable to risks associated with the variability in international trade.

Moreover, the spatial dynamics of the metropolitan growth hubs ensures that workers continue to migrate in search of employment opportunities, even if it means that there is a growth of informal settlements on the outskirts of the major metropolitan areas. Attempts to "rebalance" to smaller, more compact, interior towns, even within the more advanced provinces such as Guangdong and Zhejiang, have been less than successful (Luo and Zhu 2020; Ahmad, Niu and Xiao 2018).

The off-budget operations of the land sales proceeds have led to a lack of financial transparency, wasteful spending, and potential for rent-seeking. As part of the anti-corruption campaign and to minimize local risks, the central government in recent years clamped down on land sales as a means of financing local spending. Nonetheless, the incentives for local governments to use this instrument remain. These have intensified with the reduction in revenue shares due to the fiscal stimulus applied by the central government since 2018, accelerating during the response to the pandemic.

In China, the problems are compounded in that cities do not have recurrent revenues from property taxation and continue to rely on land sales often at the expense of farmers receiving a very much lower price than the land is worth. This, in itself, generates a vicious cycle leading to an influx of migrants looking for work.

1.2 *Taxation of Property Sales and Business Properties*

China imposes a full panoply of taxes on property sales and on businesses that very much reflect OECD practices. Table 4.1 describes the taxes and bases, and Table 4.2 summarizes the rate structures. There are several

Table 4.1 Current system of property taxation in China: tax bases

Types of taxes on land and property	*Effective date*	*Legal incidence (taxpayer)*	*Tax base*	*Assessment base*
**Urban and Township Land Use Tax (LUT)*	1988	Domestic enterprises and individuals	Area of land occupied	Area based
**House Property Tax*	1986	Domestic enterprises and individuals	Original value, if not available: comparable sales approach or rental income	Residual value (original value minus 10%–30%)
Urban Real Estate Tax (URET)	1951	Foreign enterprises. Chinese enterprises with foreign investment	• Buildings and land separately • Real estate (land and buildings) • Rent	• Standard[69] value • Consolidated standard value • Standard rental value
Farm Land Occupation Tax	1987	Domestic enterprises and individuals, foreign enterprises	Area of farmland occupied	Area based
Business Tax	1994	Entity and individuals	Transfer of land-use rights, and immovable properties (price spread between buying and sales price for buildings since 2003)	Market price
Tax on the Use of Arable Land		Entities and individuals	Arable land that is used to build houses or for other non-agricultural construction purposes	
Land Appreciation Tax	1994	All	"Appreciation amount," proceeds received at transfer stage of real estate minus (i) sum paid for land use rights, (ii) land development cost, (iii) building construction cost, (iv) taxes related to transfer of real estate	Net market value
Deed Tax	1950: revised 1997	All	Purchase, transfer, or exchange of property	Self-reported value of and houses transfer: transaction value

Table 4.2 Local tax rates set within centrally determined bands

China	Types of taxes on land and property	Tax rate	Local discretion over tax rates
	**Urban and Township Land Use Tax*	(1) Large cities: RMBY 0.5–10/m² (2) Medium-size cities: RMBY 0.4–8/m² (3) Small cities: RMBY 0.3–6/m² (4) Counties, townships, and mining districts: RMBY 0.2–4/m².	Central government sets ranges. Provinces determine range within given ranges by central government, municipalities, and counties classify land and set applicable tax rate within the range of provinces
	**House Property Tax*	The tax liability is computed as 1.2% of the original value of the property less an exemption amount ranging between 10 and 30%. For rental houses, the tax liability is 12% of rental income	
	Urban Real Estate Tax	(1) Buildings: 1% of standard value of buildings (2) Land: 1.5% of standard value of land (3) If not applicable: 1.5% of consolidated standard value (4) If not applicable: 15% standard rental value	
	Fanti Land Occupation Tax	(1) County with ≥ 1 one mu of farmland per person: 2–10 yuan/m² (2) County with 1–2 mu farmland per person: 1.6–8 yuan/m² (3) County with 2–3 mu farmland per person: 1.3–6.5 yuan/m² (4) County with ≥ 3 mu farmland per person: 1–5 yuan/m² Residents: Half of these rates are applied *One hectare equals 15 mu	County; for provinces, autonomous regions, and municipalities at provincial level the Ministry of Finance has assessed the average tax per unit (ranges from 2.5 to 9 yuan)
	Business tax	5% land and immovable/movable property (including transfer of land use rights)	
	Tax on the Use of Arable Land	The tax amount standard ranges from RMB 5 to 50/m²	
	Land appreciation tax	Progressive tax rates from 30% to 60%: (1) 30% appreciation amount not exceeding 50% of the sum of deductible items (2) 40% appreciation between 50–100% of the sum of deductible items (3) 50% appreciation between 100–200% of the sum of deductible items (4) 60% appreciation exceeding 200% of the sum of deductible items	
	Deed Tax	3–5%	Provinces determine rate within the range

sound principles underlying these taxes, that we will build on in designing a recurrent beneficial property tax that might be developed in designing an alternative to property sales—that generate the bulk of property-related revenues. Although many of the instruments in use (described in Tables 4.1 and 4.2) are appropriate, the revenues from transactions cannot be predicted with much certainty. For this reason, these cannot be effectively used as collateral for access to credit (Ahmad 2021). But there are several positive features that can be developed further in designing a more robust recurrent system of property taxation.

Businesses and foreign companies are appropriately taxed on an ownership and valuation basis (as in the UK). The base is either determined by depreciated historical cost, comparable sales, or annual rental value, as in many advanced countries. Rentals are taxed using the annual rental value mechanism.

The transfer of land use rights or properties is based on a market price-driven capital gains criterion. This is again appropriate since the absence of financing cannot be used as a criticism of the instrument. This is also one of the mechanisms for *land value capture*.

The urban and township land use tax is area based with a progressively higher rate for the bigger cities (see Table 4.2). A land appreciation tax is also applied at the transfer stage and could be seen as the equivalent of betterment levies.

A sophisticated "piggyback" arrangement is already in use, with a band set by the central government/National People Congress (NPC) (given that China is *de jure* a unitary state). A nested system is in operation, with provinces setting a sub-band within the national band. Municipalities and counties set their tax rates within the provincial band.

1.3 Alternate Options for Recurrent Taxation of Properties and Local Own-Source Revenues

As part of a continuing rationalization of the main taxes, the business tax was integrated into the VAT in the 2015 reforms, to reduce the cost of doing business and create a better integrated domestic market and trading system. An important consequence was the removal of borders around Special Economic Zones (SEZ), including particularly Shenzhen, to permit a better utilization of regional linkages. It is also the foundation for the creation of a high-tech zone, and the basis for the Greater Bay Area initiative. However, the consequence of reform was that the last major instrument of own-source revenues at the local level was eliminated, and budgetary problems began to manifest, particularly at the lower echelons within provinces (Xiao 2018).

In 2018, all sub-national tax administrations were folded into the State Tax Administration (SAT), to create synergies across tax instruments, and help to further reduce the cost of doing business. It will also make it much more difficult to engage in rent-seeking activities. It is important to note, however, that the establishment of a central tax administration for all taxes does not prevent the creation of own-source taxes at the local level. The latter depends solely on setting rates at the margin, and this is already being utilized for some of the property-related taxes in China, as seen above. A centralized tax administration is not a constraint to a "local property tax" of the "beneficial kind" as we develop further below.

The housing market across large cities in China grew rapidly after two major housing sector reforms in 1988 and 1995, respectively (Man 2011). The 1988 reform started China's housing sector privatization, with the majority of housing stock sold to SOE employees at heavily subsidized prices. The 1995 reforms set the stage for the development of a comprehensive real estate market in China, which boosted private housing ownership to about 60% by 2016.

A recurrent property tax for Chinese cities has been debated since the early 2000s. Pilots on variants of the ownership and valuation model were tried in Shanghai and Chongqing in 2011. In Shanghai, the tax was levied on second properties, and in Chongqing on valuations of properties twice the average price in the city. Neither was particularly successful, and collections were meager. Perhaps the most cogent case against the application of the ownership-valuation model was provided in a Lincoln Institute assessment that with the "lack of private ownership and absence of open markets…it is not clear what process could be used to assign a value to any parcel…and implementing a property tax will be a gradual process in China" (Bahl 2011, p. 264).

The influential Development Research Center-World Bank (DRC-WB 2014) report makes a strong case for a property tax to replace land sales and land-based financing. This is needed to provide market-based incentives to firms and households in their location and migration decisions, as the pressure on the metropolitan areas increases exponentially. Yet DRC-WB does not provide an explicit formulation for a property tax, and the implication remains that they had the typical ownership-valuation model in mind. Although recognizing that the UK generates almost 4% of the GDP in property tax, considerably above the US (2.6%) or the OECD average of 2.2% of the GDP, DRC-WB (2014) does not discuss the characteristics of the beneficial tax model (see below). Rather, given the poor performance of the ownership-valuation model in the more advanced emerging market economies, including in Latin America the DRC-WB study sets a 1% of GDP target for the property tax in China. In our view, this would not be sufficient to persuade Chinese local governments to shift away from land sales.

At least 1.5% of the GDP is needed from a formulation of the property tax if land sale financing is to be largely or fully replaced. Indeed, as argued in the following sections based on simulations for six cities, 2% of the GDP is feasible in a relatively short period of time.

There is a rapidly increasing literature on aspects of the property tax in China, including DRC-WB (2014) and Salm (2017). Dale-Johnson and Zhu (2017) and Choi and Sjoquist (2014) examine the impact of a property tax on the housing market, focusing on house price, rental cost, vacancy rate, and government revenue.

Cao and Hu (2016) focus on the distributional impact of a property tax using a theoretical model to quantify the welfare impact. They analyze the distribution impact of a property tax sensibly combined with targeted education and social housing subsidies using the 2010 China Family Panel Survey (CFPS). However, the conclusions arrived in this study are not robust because of two major data limitations: (1) the sample size for each city is too small (about 270 households) to provide meaningful distributional analysis; and (2) this sample coverage excludes migrant households. Given the large share of migrant population in metropolitan areas, and capital cities, and the majority of which have no access to social services or social housing, their exclusion from the Cao and Hu (2016) analysis misses the effects on some of the poorest and most vulnerable households—although not all migrants are poor (especially those skilled workers and entrepreneurs who move across cities)—an important qualifier as we see later.

Several additional studies have focused on land taxation and a property tax. Ding (2005) provides detailed suggestions for reforming the existing land tax system, and discusses the challenges facing the Chinese municipalities and traditional options. Anglin et al. (2014) focus on incentive issues associated with land policies. Brys et al. (2013) propose a recurrent property tax, albeit of the traditional ownership-valuation kind.

The development of a property tax system was highlighted as a reform priority for China's 14th Five-Year Plan. Additional pilots were initiated at the end of 2021.

2 Simulating a Beneficial Property Tax for China

The simulations in this chapter draw on Ahmad et al. (2021), who use a simplified area-based beneficial property tax model for recurrent taxation, as described in Chap. 1.

In China, since beneficial property tax would replace land sales, Ahmad et al. (2021) take a 2% of GDP target in each city. As we shall see, this target if applied across Chinese cities will provide considerably greater revenues per capita in the richer cities, partially offsetting the higher costs of service provision. But the creation of a significant own-source revenue base at the sub-national level will also enable sustainable access to a municipal bond system and other forms of private credit for infrastructure. It will also facilitate the effective operation of an "equalization" framework at the sub-provincial level, to provide all cities with the ability to provide similar levels of service at similar levels of tax effort—the principle of the national equalization framework (Ahmad and Searle 2006, and Lou Jiwei 1997, for the innovative Chinese equalization system).

The recurrent property tax model we develop in the next section draws on several of the key features of the taxation of property that are already in operation in China at the present time:

- Area-based tax linked to location and occupancy rather than ownership.
- A nested piggyback arrangement, where the central government sets a band, within which provinces choose a range, and municipalities and counties set a rate. For illustration purposes, we take an average rate/m^2 for a city designed to generate 2% of GDP in revenues.
- Although, a range of benefits could be estimated, including for social spending on municipal budgets, particularly basic education and social housing, Ahmad et al. (2021) simulate options that provide subsidies to migrants only or all poor residents for housing or education.

In China, the tax-benefit linkage would diffuse political resistance and lead to greater accountability for the clearer responsibilities envisaged under State Council Resolution 8/2018. It could also be made distributionally attractive, as seen in the sections below.

A simple tax on occupancy could also provide a mechanism to address special issues related to migrant informal sector workers, among the most vulnerable groups in China. The tax could be used as a mechanism to ensure access to local public services.

The current valuation-based taxation of business properties; and all sales, including residential properties, should be maintained. However, for both equity and revenue purposes, a surcharge or additional stamp duties could be imposed on properties above a specific value for both revenue and distributional purposes.

Ahmad et al. (2021) examined the distributional impact of a simplified beneficial tax on occupancy, and alternative linkages with benefit systems. Simple thought experiments or simulations are based on a sample of six cities reflecting the different urbanization challenges that are involved in a sustainable urban transition, using the 2016 China Urban Labor Surveys (CULS).

The 2016 CULS is the fourth round following those conducted in 2001, 2005, and 2010 by Institute of Population and Labor Economics, Chinese Academy of Social Sciences. The 2016 CULS covers Shanghai, and other provincial capital cities, including Guangzhou (Guangdong province, and one of the main centers for the Greater Bay Area transformation to a knowledge and innovation driven metropolitan area), Wuhan (Hubei province in the center of the country), Xian (Shaanxi province, also in the interior), Shenyang (Liaoning Province in the Rust Belt—NE of China) and Fuzhou (Fujian province along the coast). Shanghai and Guangzhou represent first tier metropolitan cities that are being transformed into more service-oriented cleaner and more compact cities. Rebalancing from exports to domestic consumption, and from the coast to the interior, requires the development of smaller interior (second tier) cities such as Wuhan. Shenyang represents a city in the "rust belt" that is losing workers and populations. In other jurisdictions in the LSE/CUT work in the program, we also look at Jieshou and Nanchang, but these cities are not covered by the CULS.

The focus of a beneficial property tax would be on transforming the major coastal metropolitan areas but also creating conditions for sustainable growth in the interior (called in the 13th and 14th Five-Year Plans: "rebalancing" and most recently "dual circulation" with a shift to domestic markets in the interior, while maintaining trade linkages). The creation of a high-tech hub in the Greater Bay Area is also contingent on strengthening local finances. Guangzhou is at the center of the Greater Bay Area initiative. Shanghai remains a premier financial and technological hub, and the corridor to Hangzhou in the Yangtze River Valley is one of the most important zones for the innovation and e-commerce transformation of urban China. The smaller, interior cities are the center of focus for the rebalancing toward a new "ecological civilization." Of course, rebalancing also involves within-province adjustments, as the inequality within Guangdong is as high as for China, so an adjustment of activities out of Guangzhou will likely involve cities within the province in the first instance (Ahmad et al. 2018).

2.1 *The Data*

One of the key objectives of the CULS is to track population movements and gain a sound understanding of how migrants have fared in large cities in comparison with the local population. Such information is intended to guide the reform of hukou system and social protection schemes to facilitate labor mobility and improve equality in access to services by gradually integrating rural-urban migrants into the urban system, as part of the New Urban Plan.

The sample design pays special attention to the migrant population, which have been largely excluded or underrepresented in many Chinese urban household surveys, including the Chinese Household Income Project (CHIP) and the Chinese Family Planning Survey (CFPS). Another strength of the CULS data is the large sample size, with about 1200 households (700 local and 500 migrant households) in Shanghai and Guangzhou and about 1000 households (600 local and 400 migrant households) in each of other cities; and the total sample size of 6400 households (3800 of local and 2600 migrant households), in comparison to CFPS which has about 280 households in each province. The survey collects a wide range of household information on social-economic conditions, education and skills, employment, access to public services and social protection schemes, and housing conditions. The top panel of Table 4.3 presents the summary data.

The statistics represent three sets of key variables from the CULS, including the distribution of sample by migration status, incomes, and housing conditions.

Table 4.3 Summary of key statistics from the CULS survey and city profiles

	Panel 1 Summary of key variables from the CULS					
	Guangzhou	*Shanghai*	*Shenyang*	*Wuhan*	*Xian*	*Fuzhou*
Sample size	3097	3046	2257	2710	2358	2642
Rural-urban migrant (%)	25.57	15.60	7.12	11.59	10.52	8.23
City-city migrant (%)	17.97	13.47	4.78	9.09	10.06	5.21
Local residence (%)	56.46	70.94	88.10	79.32	79.42	86.56
Income per capita (monthly, yuan)	3605.95	5048.33	2337.27	2680.69	2810.42	3144.21
Housing Conditions						
Sources of housing						
(1) purchase from market (%)	40.28	46.06	62.00	39.79	22.53	53.21
(2) purchase from work unit (%)	13.33	14.48	17.45	23.83	37.66	8.67
(3) rent from market (%)	30.67	24.98	10.84	15.51	23.62	19.04
(4) other sources (%)	15.71	14.49	9.71	20.87	16.18	19.08
Living space per capita (sq. meter)	25.71	26.89	29.88	29.07	31.32	33.31
Monthly rental cost per capita (yuan)	544.74	911.04	457.70	430.96	559.71	741.83
Rent as % of income	15.11	18.05	19.58	16.08	19.92	23.59
Median self-reported property value (10,000 yuan)	120.00	300.00	42.00	75.00	38.00	150.00
Source: CULS Survey made available by CASS						
	Panel 2 City profile indicators from City Statistical Yearbooks					
Socio-economic indicators	Guangzhou	Shanghai	Shenyang	Wuhan	Xian	Fuzhou
Population in 2016 (million)	14.0	24.2	8.3	10.8	8.8	7.6
Share of migrants in 2016 (%)	38.0	40.1	11.4	22.5	6.6	9.2
Migrant growth rate during 2010–5 (%)	6.7	9.2	8.5	63.2	-15.1	9.2
GDP per capita in 2016	139,192	116,562	66,893	111,469	71,647	82,251
Public Finance (2016)						
Revenue (hundred million yuan)	2218	6406	621	1322	641	599

(continued)

Table 4.3 (continued)

	Panel 1 Summary of key variables from the CULS					
	Guangzhou	*Shanghai*	*Shenyang*	*Wuhan*	*Xian*	*Fuzhou*
(1) Revenue per cap (excluding migrants) (10,000 yuan)	25,485	44,180	8455	15,855	7771	8717
(2) Revenue per cap (local + migrant) (10,000 yuan)	15,797	26,475	7489	12,280	7258	7912
Expenditure (hundred million yuan)	2845	6919	825	1525	943	830
(1) Exp per cap (excluding migrant) (10,000 yuan)	32,690	47,717	11,239	18,285	11,425	12,079
(2) Exp per cap (local + migrant) (10,000 yuan)	20,263	28,594	9954	14,162	10,672	10,963
Financing Gap (10,000 yuan)						
Rev (1) -Exp (1) with no migrants	-7204	-3537	-2784	-2429	-3654	-3362
Rev (2) -Exp (2) with migrants	-4465	-2119	-2466	-1882	-3413	-3052
Public services						
No. of student enrollment (primary)/10,000	1113	326	509	603	641	754
No. of student enrollment (普通中学)/10,000	581	236	364	370	320	431
No. of hospitals/10,000	0.3	0.2	0.4	0.4	0.4	0.2
No. of doctors/10,000	53.8	45.2	26.6	41.6	33.8	15.6
Share of pension covered (%)	55.2	69.3	29.9	25.5	37.4	22.3
Share of medical care (%)	45.3	69.8	40.8	36.4	49.3	20.5
Share of unemployment insurance (%)	35.8	66.7	16.9	17.9	17.3	15.8
Land use						
Ratio of investment in real estate (2000 to 2016)	7.1	6.6	11.1	24.9	37.7	22.1

Source: City Statistical Yearbooks

Note: As Shanghai is a metropolitan area with provincial status, it receives also shared revenues as a province—distinguishing it from other capital cities in the sample that do not have the same status

2.2 *What Does the Data Tell Us About the Six Cities?*

Guangzhou is the most diverse city with the highest proportion of migrants, with rural-urban migrants accounting for about one quarter of the city population, city migrants to Guangzhou about 17%. Local households with Hukou represent about half of the sample. In contrast, the sample in Shenyang and Fuzhou is dominated by local households which accounted for over 85% of sampled households.

Not all migrants to Fuzhou are poor, and some may be better off than older residents, particularly those who have retired or are on fixed income salaries.

The group of income-poor families living in relatively valuable properties poses a significant political-economy challenge to the operation of the traditional valuation-based property tax. The comparison of the sample distribution by migration status with the share of migrants from the population census (presented in panel 2 of Table 4.3) confirms that the household sample for all six cities is accurately representative of the population structure stratified by migration status. The cross-city comparison confirms that Shanghai ranks highest in per capita income, followed by Guangzhou, although the latter has a higher per capita GDP. However, both cities have much smaller average living space per capita, compared with other four cities. This reflects both the population density of these metropolitan areas, as well as the higher cost of housing and public services.

Guangzhou, however, displays both urban sprawl and inefficient land use, largely driven by the dependence on land sales financing, compared with other metropolitan areas such as Seoul. The majority of households in Shenyang live in properties purchased from market (62%), with only 10% of households in the sample relying on rental properties. In contrast, Guangzhou had the largest rental market (about a third of households lived in rental properties), followed by Shanghai (a quarter), Xian (23%), and Fuzhou (19%).

Panel 2 of Table 4.3 presents city profile indicators constructed from the China City Statistical Yearbook. It is interesting to note that while Shanghai and Guangzhou have a higher level of concentration of migrants, Wuhan saw the largest increase of in migrant inflows. On the other hand, Xian experienced a reduction of migrants over the period of 2010–5. This presents a mixed picture with respect to the changing nature of migration to cities in the interior, consistent with Luo and Zhu (2020).

There is a significant disparity in public finances across the six cities, with Shanghai having the largest revenue per capita, followed by Guangzhou and Wuhan. As noted above, the Shanghai financing is not comparable with the other cities as it has the status of a province and also receives province-related revenue shares. At the lower end, Shenyang, Xian, or **Fuzhou**, have revenue per capita less than one-fifth that of Shanghai, but also lower than Guangzhou or Wuhan.

On the other hand, the per capita financing gap, measured by the difference between revenue and spending, is relatively similar in magnitude across all cities, except for Guangzhou which has a much larger deficit than the others and also stands out in several key indicators.

First, Guangzhou's fiscal deficit was extremely large, about twice the average across six cities. However, second, its public services provision in education and health ranked high, with the highest student enrolment in primary and middle schools and the number of doctors per 10,000 population. Third, Guangzhou also had a good record of social welfare coverage, ranking second after Shanghai. Guangzhou warrants an in-depth analysis to examine the sources of fiscal imbalances, which can provide important lessons for other cities. It is noteworthy that Guangzhou had the highest per capita GDP of all the cities, so a property tax as a constant percentage of GDP would give a much-needed boost to Guangzhou's budget financing difficulties.

Land sales financing has had a major impact on local developments, but with the downside of urban sprawl, loss of prime agricultural land and wetlands in the deltas, as well as potential price bubbles that have proved problematic in Hong Kong. An instruction to restrict land sales was offset by the reductions in shared revenues as national tax rates on broad-based taxes were reduced. Consequently, in the three cities, including Guangzhou, surveyed in Ahmad and Niu, there has been a resumption of land sales financing of local spending. This is also seen in Xian, Fuzhou, and Shenyang.

The case of Wuhan is interesting. It has grown rapidly during the post-2010 period to become a high-tech and manufacturing hub, or "Chicago" of China, and the city has grown to be bigger than the Greater London Area (11 m people) in the center of the country, with excellent high-speed train, motorway, and connectivity as well as modern airports. There has been a phenomenal increase in migrants (Table 4.3, panel 2), and these are at both ends of the income scale—with highly skilled workers and entrepreneurs, as well as the "floating" population or informal sector workers. Given the emphasis on new infrastructure, Wuhan had more hospital beds per capita than Shanghai, but the increasing budgetary pressures over the recent past have squeezed preventive care facilities.

The different socio-economic conditions, in particular housing, as well as the varying degree of concentration of the migrant population across the six cities provide an important opportunity to investigate the impact of alternatve policy options. More importantly, the data allow us to address the key political economy issues, that is, how different social groups could be affected by alternative policy proposals. This then provides the basis to develop a reform package that can balance the interests of different groups, including all residents in the jurisdiction, with or without Hukou status, as well as across different socio-economic groups, to ensure broader support and social cohesion.

2.3 *The Political Economy Constraints*

The socio-economic and demographic characteristics of the population play a key role in shaping the political implications as result of the differential policy impact across various groups within the jurisdiction. Consequently, a tax reform is likely to be subject to more political constraints in cities with a more diverse population structure because of the need to balance different interest groups. Guangzhou presents a case in point. Among the six cities, it has the highest concentration of migrant households. The analysis of different social groups using Guangzhou as the case study (see Ahmad 2018) provides important insights into the political economy implications of the reform, serving as the upper bound benchmark for other cities with less heterogeneity.

Three key features are most prominent in China's decades of urbanization, including (1) population migration (both from rural to urban areas and across cities) at an unprecedented scale, (2) high income and wealth inequality within cities, and (3) a rapidly aging urban population that has increased demand for social services often provided by migrant workers.

Regrouping the households by migration status and income level can be a useful approach to gain an insight into how different interest groups could be affected by the reform proposal, and the political economy implications. In addition, it is also important to analyze how demographics, in particular the concentration of children of school age and the elderly, vary across these groups. Such information is critical to inform policy design relating to social spending, such as education and social care, to develop a more balanced and equitable reform package, reaching all segments of the population within the revenue envelope. Two key questions can be addressed using the household survey data.

First, how do demographics and socio-economic conditions vary across households of different migration status? Table 4.4 presents a summary of three household groups defined as (1) rural-urban migrants, (2) city-city migrants, and (3) local residents. On demographics, there is a parity in the number of school children across households of different migration status (possibly as a result of family planning policies), but the elderly are concentrated more among local households. Thus, a policy favoring migrant children might provide higher benefits to better-off households than local retirees (this seems to be picked up in some of our simulations, e.g., for Fuzhou—see below).

Rural-urban migrants are usually the most economically disadvantaged, with lowest average incomes, relying on rental properties with rental cost

Table 4.4 Population profile of Guangzhou by income

	Lowest	*2rd*	*3rd*	*4th*	*Top*	*Total*
Migration status (%)						
Rural-GZ (%)	35.7	30.9	30.3	18.3	13.0	25.7
Other city-GZ (%)	18.5	15.6	11.4	21.4	21.8	17.8
Local GZ (%)	45.8	53.5	58.3	60.3	65.1	56.6
All households	100	100	100	100	100	100
Demographics						
No. of school age children	0.44	0.33	0.30	0.17	0.23	0.28
No. of elderly (aged 60 and above)	0.30	0.24	0.38	0.50	0.27	0.34
Income per capita (monthly)	999	2013	2921	3992	8122	3606
Housing condition						
Housing Sources						
(1) purchase from market	32.8	32.4	42.9	51.7	41.7	40.3
(2) purchase from work unit	6.7	8.1	12.4	14.9	24.6	13.3
(3) rent from market	39.5	38.9	29.1	22.0	23.6	30.7
(4) other sources	21.0	20.5	15.6	11.4	10.1	15.7
All options	100	100	100	100	100	100
Living space per capita (sq m)	22.2	19.8	24.1	29.4	32.9	25.7
Monthly rental cost per capita (yuan)	418.5	369.3	537.3	699.0	964.3	544.7
Rental cost as % of monthly income (%)	41.9	18.3	18.4	17.5	11.9	15.1
Median self-reported property value (10,000 yuan)	80.0	80.0	102.0	150.0	200.0	120.0

Source: Ahmad et al. (2021)

accounting for a larger share of monthly income. The living space per capita of rural migrants is about 70% that of their local counterparts (not considering housing quality), but there is little disparity in living space between city migrants and the locals. The comparison of housing conditions indicates that rising housing prices can have a large adverse impact on housing security among rural migrants. Investing in affordable social housing in large cities should be set as a priority to address economic insecurity. This has been taken up in Shenzhen as the Hong Kong-based model is being questioned.

Table 4.4 presents (for Guangzhou) a comparison of a broader set of socio-economic indicators across these three groups of households and their changes among rural-urban migrants using the 2010 and 2016 CULS. The rural-urban migrant workers are disproportionally concentrated in low-skilled, low-paid, and informal sector jobs and largely excluded from government/state-owned firms, which generally offer more job security and better social insurance and benefits.

The trend analysis shows that while some progress had been made in expanding the coverage of social insurance to rural-urban migrants between 2010 and 2016, only a third of migrant workers were covered in the social insurance scheme by 2016. Yet, not all migrant workers are poor—and city-to-city migrants are typically well educated and more entrepreneurial, and likely to be among the better-off groups. This can complicate targeting solely by migration categorization. Similar data are available for the other cities.

The second question concerns how key demographic and housing conditions vary across income groups in a metropolitan area like Guangzhou. Children of school age are concentrated more among low-income groups, but the elderly are largely concentrated in the two middle income groups. As expected, rural-urban migrants are disproportionally concentrated in the bottom income group, and city-to-city migrants tend to be better skilled and fit into the upper income groups (Table 4.5).

The bottom income group lives in more crowded properties in Guangzhou (Table 4.4), with per capita living space (22 sq m) being about 70% of the top income group, and the rental cost accounted for about 40% of their monthly income, compared with 10% among the top income group. Among households in the bottom of the income distribution, about 32% of households lived in properties purchased from market, 7% purchased from work units, and 40% from rental properties, in comparison to the top income groups, at 41%, 25%, and 23%, respectively.

Table 4.5 Population profile of Guangzhou (GZ) by migration status

	Rural to GZ	*Other city to GZ*	*Local*	*Total*
Migration status (%)	25.6	18.0	56.5	100.0
Demographics				
No. of school children	0.3	0.3	0.2	0.3
No. of elderly (aged 60 and above)	0.1	0.1	0.5	0.3
Income per capita (Yuan per month)	2943.5	3716.9	3871.6	3605.9
Housing condition				
Housing Sources				
(1) purchase from market	17.2	41.0	50.3	40.3
(2) purchase from work unit	1.0	3.1	22.0	13.3
(3) rent from market	74.8	48.8	5.5	30.7
(4) other sources	7.1	7.1	22.2	15.7
All options	100.0	100.0	100.0	100.0
Living space per capita (sq. m)	20.6	27.9	27.3	25.7
Monthly rental cost per capita (yuan)	483.1	776.6	416.0	544.7
Rental cost as % of monthly income (%)	16.4	20.9	10.7	15.1
Median of estimated property value (10,000 yuan)	100.0	110.0	125.0	120.0

The fact that nearly a quarter of the top income groups were able to purchase property from work units (often at heavily discounted prices), highlights an aspect of China's rapid increase in wealth inequality. The *wealth Gini coefficient increased from 0.34 in 1988 to 0.79* in 2018 (WEF 2018), which some argue was driven in part by the privatization of the housing sector and the liberalization of capital markets, accompanied by a sharp increase in asset prices (Piketty et al. 2017).[1]

The population profile analysis reveals important political-economy implications of the proposed reforms. It identifies the potential differential welfare impact of the reform both across key stakeholders and across socio-economic groups. Shenyang is a rust belt city struggling to upgrade the old industrial base dominated by SOEs, and is a less attractive destination for migrants, with the lowest concentration of rural migrants. Guangzhou is the most diverse and attractive for migrants from rural and other urban areas, and all skill levels. The political constraints of the reform

[1] The private housing stock surged from about 60% in 1978 to over 95% in 2015, and the capital market with private ownership of domestic equities rose to about 30% in 2015 from near zero in 1978.

in Shenyang could be very different from that in Guangzhou, given the homogeneity of the population (local households account for almost 90% of the sample households in the former). On the other hand, the political economy narrative for the other cities could be somewhere in between the two extreme cases.

2.4 The Simulations

Ahmad et al. (2021) examine the effects of a recurrent beneficial property tax using a simple design based on area, location, and occupancy. Political opposition is reduced with the direct linkage to benefits, for example, for education or social housing. The local setting of rates within a centrally determined band (already in place for taxation of property sales) is important in creating a stable own-source revenue source, and this is critical for reducing risks associated with the buildup of local liabilities (Ahmad 2021). Also, an objective of the reform is to make it more attractive for lower-income and less skilled workers to move to cheaper, interior cities, and the beneficial property tax can play a signaling role in this context.

In China, the area-based beneficial approach is a suitable option because of the complexity of the housing stock (a large share of privatized public housing stock from previous SOEs and public sector units were made available on a restricted leasehold basis) and possible distortion of property valuations given the extensive involvement of local governments in property development. The property value information collected in the 2016 survey is based on households' own assessments, which can be highly unreliable because of the complexity discussed above. For example, many properties bought from the previous SOEs at heavily discounted prices often were in premium locations, but they could not be freely traded in the property market due to complexity of ownership titles. While the purchase price is an underestimate of the value of the property, there is no effective free market price either.

The following analysis adopts the area-based assessment method for a property tax and distributional impacts of alternative formulations of the proposal are illustrated through policy simulations using the CULS data for the six cities. Although positive effects on income distribution would be more marked by targeting migrant and low-income households, overall political acceptability is increased if all the population were to benefit from the tax (see Ahmad 2018). Also, it is likely that in China, the beneficial property tax revenues will flow to municipal budgets and then to basic spending requirements such as education or health care that are provided free, and hence do not appear in household surveys. While the policy simulations use measurable variables, the main objective of a "beneficial" property tax is precisely to ensure that the city/county government pays attention to say "preventive health care" (as in Wuhan), for which there is also broad public support.

The distributional impact analysis is carried out using a policy simulation exercise; and to focus on the "gainers and losers" story we assume that the entire beneficial property tax revenue is distributed for specific benefit. We assess distributional consequences sequentially to illustrate the individual as well as the combined effect of a property tax and social spending on income inequality. This involves the construction of three income variables. The "initial income" (Y_0) is the recorded household income, net of income tax, and social security contribution; the "disposable income" (Y_d) is estimated after deducting a property tax; and the "final income" (Y_f) is constructed by adding social transfers (education and housing subsidies) to Y_d.

Key steps and assumptions imposed in the simulations are as follows. The first step focuses on setting a tax rate. In theory, a city-specific property tax rate should be set based on the principles of equity, administrative simplicity, and fiscal sustainability. In the latter case, local governments should set the rate to reflect their assessment of spending needs (proposed services) and associated costs. For simplicity, Ahmad et al. (2021) estimate the tax rate under the assumption that all cities set the rate to raise local revenue to a level of 2% of the local GDP, to provide somewhat more revenues than land sales that would be phased out.

In the second step, child/education transfers are estimated for each city based on current city-level per capita education spending (see Table 4.6).[2] All migrant households with children of school age are provided with transfers. In a second iteration, we allocate funds for all children as a form of child benefit (this is appropriate since all cities run deficits, and education spending in particular presents financing difficulties for cities with mandates and no own-source revenues, e.g., Nanchang). Finally, all low-income households, defined as those with per capita incomes below 50% of the city-level median income, are provided with transfers for education or housing.

[2] The method for estimating the benefit from public education spending consists of imputing a value to the benefit accrued to an individual of going to public schools that equals the per-beneficiary input costs obtained from administrative data for individual cities.

Table 4.6 Simulations of property tax 2% of GDP, and educational spending

City	*Property tax 2% GDP (Υ bn)*	*Current education spending (Υ bn)*	*Property tax (Υ)/ m²*
Guangzhou	39.2	32.12	121.4
Shanghai	54.9	84.10	90.81
Shenyang	10.9	11.51	52.68
Wuhan	23.8	23.11	85.11
Xian	12.5	11.96	48.8
Fuzhou	12.4	15.31	54.6

Source: Ahmad, Niu, Wang and Wang (2021)

It is interesting that the 2% of GDP level more or less covers the education spending in each of the capital cities, other than Shanghai, which is a metropolitan city with provincial status and thus also benefits from a full share of the VAT (thus higher than the other capital cities). The considerably greater spending on education also probably explains the very strong performance of Shanghai in the Global Pisa rankings.

The assessment of the distributional consequences is based on the two most commonly used inequality measures—the Gini coefficient and Atkinson index (A).[3] While the Gini coefficient is the more widely used index, it is most sensitive to income changes in the middle segment of the income distribution. This typically reflects preferences of policy makers in a large number of countries. The Atkinson index permits the weights on different segments of the distribution of income to vary from 0 (zero), where equal weights are given to all segments of the population and no preference to any group, to higher values, say, on the impact on poorer groups. Inequality aversion parameters of 0.5 to 1 reflect the preferences of most distributionally inclined governments and more or less mirror the Gini coefficient. To focus on the lowest end of the size distribution, we also use an inequality aversion parameter of 2, for the Atkinson index. This focuses attention on poorer households, such as migrants in most cities. But one must be careful, as not all migrants are poor. From Table 4.5, we see in Guangzhou that migrants from other cities have more or less the

[3] The Atkinson index allows different weights on relative positions in the income distribution, given by a coefficient, labeled as e, that reflects the level of "inequality aversion." The greater the weight on the inequality aversion parameter, the more sensitive Atkinson index (e) is to income differences at the bottom of the distribution. Common choices of e range from 0 to 2, where 0 implies that a yuan to the poorest is treated the same as a yuan to the richest (zero inequality aversion), and 2 puts almost exclusive weight on the poorest.

same per capita incomes as residents and are equally likely to have above-average living space, considerably higher than the poorest groups that might include migrants from rural areas.

Table 4.7 presents the initial distributional impact for three scenarios of policy changes for six cities which result in different distributional impacts (income levels Y_j):

A_0 and G_0 at initial level Y_0;
A_1 and G_1 with the imposition of an area-based property tax (Y_1);
A_2 and G_2 with property tax combined with education subsidies (Y_2) ;
A_3 and G_3 with a property tax combined with education and social housing subsidies (Y_3).

The variance in tax rates by city provides a system of market-based incentives to limit migration to the mega-metropolises along the coast. On its own, the tax has no impact on the Gini coefficient G_j relative to the

Table 4.7 Distributional impact of the beneficial property tax options

	Atkinson index (Aj)				*Gini coefficient (Gj)*			
	Y_0	Y_1	Y_2	Y_3	Y_0	Y_1	Y_2	Y_3
GuangZhou	0.60	0.76	0.75	0.74	0.39	0.40	0.40	0.39
ShangHai	0.72	0.51	0.49	0.44	0.40	0.41	0.40	0.40
ShenYang	0.63	0.49	0.49	0.45	0.33	0.34	0.34	0.33
WuHan	0.52	0.48	0.48	0.60	0.33	0.35	0.34	0.34
XiAn	0.47	0.58	0.51	0.41	0.35	0.36	0.35	0.35
FuZhou	0.51	0.89	0.90	0.89	0.36	0.37	0.37	0.37
	Atkinson index (Aj)				Gini coefficient (Gj)			
	Y_0	Y_1	Y_2	Y_3	Y_0	Y_1	Y2	Y3
Guangzhou	0.60	0.76	0.76	0.74	0.39	0.40	0.40	0.40
Shanghai	0.72	0.51	0.50	0.46	0.40	0.41	0.41	0.40
Shenyang	0.63	0.49	0.48	0.44	0.33	0.34	0.33	0.33
Wuhan	0.52	0.48	0.47	0.59	0.33	0.35	0.34	0.34
Xian	0.47	0.58	0.49	0.39	0.35	0.36	0.35	0.35
Fuzhou	0.51	0.89	0.55	0.54	0.36	0.37	0.37	0.37

Source: Ahmad, Niu, Wang and Wang, 2021

Notes: The simulation is under the assumption of providing education (Y1) and housing (Y2) subsidies only to migrant households; The simulation is under the assumption of providing subsidies to education (Y1) and housing (Y2) all low-income households

status quo G_0 in each case, although the introduction of a housing benefit in addition to the social benefit reduces inequality in Shanghai. The Gini coefficient is more reflective of changes in the middle ranges of the income distribution and reflects the "middle class" outcomes that typically drive the political economy responses. The reform itself does not pose significant problems from this perspective, and any negative impact is completely offset with the "beneficial" linkages.

A different inequality measurement index can focus on the effects of the tax alone on the poorest groups. The Atkinson index with a relatively high inequality aversion parameter ($e = 2$), places greater weight on the bottom end of the size distribution. Here there are different impacts, probably reflecting the weight of the migrant populations in each of the metropolitan areas. In Shanghai and Shenyang, the tax alone reduces the Atkinson index significantly (see Y_1 relative to Y_0 in Table 4.7). The Wuhan case is of particular interest—where there was a huge increase in migrants in Wuhan during 2010–5, see Table 4.3 (Panel 2), both at the lower end of the income spectrum and also among the higher income groups. The influence of the latter is seen in the imposition of the tax relative to the status quo—it reduces inequality. But the targeting of migrants also includes rich households, so the provision of a benefit to migrants in this case *actually increases* inequality. This is not the case in most other cities. But it does point to the need for care in establishing the benefit criteria linked to the benefit tax.

There is no major negative distributional impact of the beneficial property tax and the provision of a housing subsidy to poor households in strongly redistributive. Shenzhen is focusing on social housing and an interface with the income tax/benefit system is desirable. Giving local exemptions could give rise to the "game play and corruption" that bedevils the property tax in many emerging market countries and should be avoided (Ahmad et al. 2015).

3 Implementing a Beneficial Property Tax in Guangzhou

A major problem in Guangzhou is that the budget has fixed and increasing spending requirements on basic services and debt financing, but the bulk of revenues are shares of national collections. The recent rational counter-cyclical policies of the central government to offset economic downturns and trade shocks has a negative impact on the Metropolitan Area's budget envelope, forcing the Guangzhou administration to revert to land sales, despite the guidance to phase out this form of financing. Although the focus in this paper is on the beneficial property tax, Ahmad (2018) has argued also to extend the "piggyback" principle on the personal income tax (PIT), with SAT administration. This would also establish a desirable link between the city-level taxation of fixed assets and the information needed to grow the PIT base. A second benefit is that if any rebates or benefits are applied in the Guangzhou context to the beneficial property tax, these can be offset against the sums due against the PIT piggyback (the rebates could also be applied to the current PIT share).

Ahmad et al. (2021) also examine the budgets of Guangzhou districts, focusing mainly on education expenditures, and assume that revenues from the beneficial property tax will accrue fully to the metropolitan area, and any distributional issues with fixed or low-income households will be addressed through the income tax-benefit system, as in the UK—either to the current PIT share or an eventual Guangzhou piggyback on the PIT. An examination of the budgets of Guangzhou's 11 districts is instructive (Table 4.8).

A 2% of GDP property tax would generate more than enough revenues (Y39 bn) to cover education spending in all districts (Y24.01 bn). But

Table 4.8 Applying the property tax in Guangzhou districts to financing education (2016 data)

RMB billion

Districts	*2% GDP property tax*	*Education spending*	*Surplus/deficit in financing*
Tianhe	7.60	2.43	5.18
Huangpu	6.01	2.17	3.84
Yuexiu	5.82	2.03	3.79
Panyu	3.51	2.69	0.81
Baiyun	3.28	2.66	0.63
Haizhu	3.10	2.08	1.02
Nansha	2.56	1.00	1.56
Huadu	2.34	2.24	0.10
Liwan	2.16	2.35	(0.19)
Zengcheng	2.09	2.63	(0.53)
Conghua	0.75	1.73	(0.98)

Source: Guangzhou, Final Accounts 2016, for all 11 districts

there is insufficient funding in the poorest three districts, and just about enough in five others. The bulk of the surplus would be generated in three of the richest districts and would also permit expansion of the remit to social housing, say. However, this would require a within-Guangzhou equalization mechanism to permit all districts to finance a similar level of service delivery at the same level of tax effort.

Thus, with a metropolitan-level equalization function, it should be possible to fund all education and increase that in the poorer districts and also anchor other activities such as access to private finance for public investments consistent with a sustainable growth strategy.

4 The Next Steps in Property Tax Reforms in China

A recurrent property tax is needed in China to finance basic services without risk of revenue fluctuation that accompanies shared revenues, and to replace the excessive local reliance on land sales. This would also help in providing the basis for a sustainable access to credit for local infrastructure, including a municipal bond system without undue risks, and the long-term buildup of liabilities through PPPs. China already has several appropriate instruments to tax property transactions. These provide directions for the alternatives for recurrent taxation, including an area-based approach differentiated by location, and the possibility of a piggybacked arrangement.

Some of the current practices that should continue include the following:

- Taxes on property sales should be maintained and would typically be supplemented by a stamp duty (with a surcharge on very expensive properties).
- Business properties should continue to be subject to an ownership-valuation-based tax, as there are generally more business-related transactions than for household property, and the same political economy considerations do not apply. This makes it possible to apply betterment levies on business properties, a much more efficient mechanism for financing local infrastructure than land sales.

- VAT should apply to all first sales, to reduce the construction costs for businesses, and to provide information on profits and wages in the construction sector.

It is important to freeze the practice of local government reliance on land sales in the Hong Kong model. This leads to urban sprawl, and rising housing costs as developers try and recoup their investments. The off-budget operations and associated PPPs have led to uncertain generation of liabilities and possibilities of rent-seeking behavior.

Ahmad et al. (2021) show that an area-based tax on occupancy designed to raise 2% of GDP would help to offset the loss of land sales revenues, and not have a negative impact on income distribution. There is no change in the Gini coefficient, and a reduction in the Atkinson index, especially with the combination of social benefit and housing subsidies to the poor. The higher taxes in the more advanced metropolitan areas relative to the smaller cities would help in providing price signals to firms and workers to relocate more labor-intensive activities to interior CCCs as part of the government's reinforced rebalancing strategy in the period of recovery from the pandemic.

The close linkage of a municipal bond system with a robust property tax regime is perhaps the most critical aspect of the reforms. It will help to reduce risk, and also facilitate a transparent access to sustainable finance for longer-term growth.

Unlike a systemic reform as with the VAT and revenue-sharing, it is possible to pilot a beneficial property tax. The pilots could be designed with a view to examining issues for mega-metropolitan areas, as well as CCCs in the interior that will be the focus of the rebalancing in the recovery from the pandemic and possible trade disruptions.

The simplified property tax would also provide an opportunity to utilize the powers of blockchain technology. This would provide for a distributed ledger that provides timely information to both local and central governments and will facilitate the functional management of information by the SAT at a central level that is also needed for the income taxes. It would also simplify both the revenue and treasury circuits, with potential benefits also for the governance institutions and processes at all levels of government.

References

Ahmad, E., (2018), "Rebalancing in China—Fiscal Policies for sustainable Growth," Singapore Economic Review, 2018, 63(4), 861-884.

Ahmad, E., (2021), "Multilevel financing of sustainable infrastructure in China—Policy options for inclusive, resilient and green growth". Journal of Infrastructure, Policy and Development, April.

Ahmad E, and R Searle, (2006) On the implementation of transfers to subnational governments. In: Ahmad and Brosio (eds) Handbook of Fiscal Federalism, Edward Elgar, Cheltenham

Ahmad E, K. Li, T. Richardson, (2002) Recentralization in China? In: Ahmad Tanzi (ed) Managing Fiscal Decentralization, Routledge

Ahmad E, Rydge J, and Stern N., (2013) Structural change drives tax reforms drives structural change, LSE, presented at the China Development Forum.

Ahmad E, G Brosio and C Pöschl, (2015) Local property taxes and benefits in developing countries: overcoming political resistance? In: Ahmad E, and Brosio G (eds) Handbook of Multilevel Finance. Edward Elgar, Cheltenham

Ahmad, E., M. Niu and K. Xiao, (2018) Fiscal Policies for Sustainable Development in China—Rebalancing in Guangdong, Springer.

Ahmad, E., Meili Niu, Liming Wang, Meiyan Wang, 2021. "Designing Beneficial Property Taxation for Sustainable Development in China—evidence from six cities, including Guangzhou" LSE Program on Financing Sustainable Urban Transitions in China and Mexico.

Anglin, Paul M., David Dale-Johnson, Yanmin Gao, and Guozhong Zhu, (2014) "Patterns of Growth in Chinese Cities: Implications of the Land Lease," Journal of Urban Economics, 2014, 83 (C), 87–107.

Bahl, R., (2011), "Intergovernmental fiscal relations in local public finance," in Man, Joyce and Y-H Hong, (2011), China's Local Public Finance in Transition, Cambridge, Massachusetts: Lincoln Institute of Land Policy.

Brys, Bert, Stephen Matthews, Richard Herd, and Xiao Wang, (2013), "Tax Policy and Tax Reform in the Peoples Republic of China," **OECD Taxation Working Papers**, No. 18, OECD Publishing, Paris.

Cao, Jing and Wenhao Hu, (2016), "A Microsimulation of Property Tax Policy in China," Journal of Housing Economics.

Choi, Ki-Whan and David L. Sjoquist, (2014), "Economic and Spatial Effects of Land Value Taxation in an Urban Area: An Urban Computable General Equilibrium Approach," Land Economics, 91, 536–555.

Dale-Johnson, David, Guozhong Zhu (2017), "Transition to the Property Tax in China: A Dynamic General Equilibrium Analysis", Working Paper WP17DD1, Lincoln Institute of Land Policy.

Development Research Center (DRC) of the State Council and the World Bank, 2014, Urban China: toward efficient, inclusive and sustainable urbanization, World Bank, Washington DC.

Ding, Chengri, (2005) "Property Tax Development in China," Land Lines, 17:3.

Lou Jiwei (1997), "Constraints in reforming the Transfer System in China," in Ahmad, E., ed., Financing Decentralized Expenditures: An international comparison of grants," Edward Elgar, 1997.

Luo X, and Zhu N., (2020) Migration, City attractiveness and Regional Hubs in China, LSE/CUT Program on Financing Sustainable Urban Transitions in China and Mexico.

Man, Joyce, (2011), "Local Public Finance in China: An Overview," in Joyce Yanyun Man and Yu-Hung Hong, eds., 2011, China's Local Public Finance in Transition, Cambridge, Massachusetts: Lincoln Institute of Land Policy.

Piketty T, Yang L, and Zucman G., (2017) Capital Accumulation, Private Property and Rising Inequality in China, 1978-2015, WID.world Working Paper Series N° 2017/6

Salm, M., (2017), Property tax in BRICS megacities, Springer.

Wang, Wen, Alfred Wu and F. Ye (2018) "Land use reforms: towards sustainable development in China," in Ahmad, Niu and Xiao (eds) op cit.

WEF (World Economic Forum). (2018), The Inclusive Growth and Development Report.

Xiao K., (2018) Managing subnational liability for sustainable development: a case study of Guangdong, in Ahmad, Niu and Xiao (2018), op cit.

Zhi Liu (2018) Land-Based Finance and Property Tax in China, ATI Working Paper.

CHAPTER 5

Mexico: Failure of the Traditional Property Tax and Proposed Beneficial Property Tax Alternative

Abstract Mexico has had a US-style ownership-valuation model property tax for a very long time, with a betterment levy, but collections are poor, and the betterment levy is dysfunctional. A significant portion of the revenues are generated in the large metro areas, particularly Mexico City. Value capture mechanism in Mexico City has improved the historical center but pushed the informal sector further into the urban sprawl, extending into the State of Mexico. The disparities in revenue generation are reflected in the service delivery differentials with respect to lagging regions. This leads to continued migrations to the metro areas, and Mexico City is sinking—almost as fast as Jakarta—and cannot take more migrants. As in the Chinese case, simulations show that a beneficial property tax could raise revenues quickly, and anchor more effective local service delivery and access to private finance to support a sustainable growth strategy to complement the connectivity investments aimed at the lagging Southern States.

Keywords Growth from below • Beneficial-tax simulation • Setting tax rates locally

This chapter draws on Ahmad, E and H. Viscarra, 2020

E. Ahmad, G. Brosio, *Beneficial Property Taxation for Emerging Market Countries*, https://doi.org/10.1007/978-3-031-08612-0_5

Why are Mexican property tax revenues so low? Rates tend to be very low, cadastral values (the base for the property tax) tend to be far below market values or missing altogether, exemptions abound, and non-compliance with payments is not sanctioned. Moreover, there is a problem with asset-rich but fixed-income households that would not be able to absorb market-based property taxes. The reasons why these issues have been neglected are to some degree due to a lack of resources but they are essentially political. Municipal governments have very little incentives to change this situation. It is far easier to receive revenues from common pool resources (high-level government transfers) than to inconvenience the electorate by collecting a highly visible tax. Even when municipal governments make an attempt to raise revenues, their efforts are sometimes blocked by the states or their powerful constituents.

1 Overview of the Property Tax

The property tax (***impuesto predial***) is the most important municipal level tax, comprising around 60% of municipal tax revenues and 30% of own revenues on average. There is much variation among Mexico's approximately 2400 municipalities. More than a third of the total property tax revenue was collected in Mexico City (CDMX) alone in 2020. In CDMX, for example, local residents pay considerably more in property tax than in Chiapas or Oaxaca (see Table 5.1 for a comparison of property tax revenues between the Federal Entities). A large number of the municipalities (around 20%) do not charge any property tax at all (or at least do not report any collections). In contrast, around 80% of the total property tax in Mexico is collected by just 100 municipalities (4%). The rest is spread out in between these extremes.

The property tax is generally considered a progressive tax, as ownership tends to be concentrated among the rich. Given that real property is immovable, it allows different municipalities to set their own rates (but not yet in Mexico) without leading to the magnitude of tax competition or relocation effects of other taxes such as the income tax or the VAT. It is further considered an appropriate tax for the municipal level as its value is (at least in part) a reflection of municipal services, such as water and drainage, street cleaning, garbage collection, road maintenance, and public lighting. As Tiebout (1956) explains, this link gives the local government incentives to provide adequate public goods that maximize property

Table 5.1 Property taxes by state, 2020

	2020			
Entidad	*Property tax*	*Immovable propertytax*	*Population*	*Catastral value / market value (in %)*
National	78,696,769,458	46,578,814,939	126,014,024	39.3
Aguascalientes	674,753,993	385,450,205	1,425,007	28.4
Baja California	1,787,856,811	1,112,436,571	3,769,020	47.6
Baja California Sur	1,077,658,784	649,373,964	798,447	40.0
Campeche	138,749,795	118,095,218	928,363	34.5
Coahuila de Zaragoza	1,631,576,915	980,401,305	3,146,771	48.6
Colima	560,898,758	277,716,743	731,391	31.0
Chiapas	573,034,422	446,025,571	5,543,828	10.4
Chihuahua	49,317,775	35,023,071	3,741,869	43.0
Cludad de México	28,539,318,600	17,499,726,300	9,209,944	na
Durango	623,560,059	445,020,237	1,832,650	6.8
Guanajuato	2,675,134,452	2,028,643,336	6,166,934	34.4
Guerrero	634,802,605	367,214,710	3,540,685	20.5
Hidalgo	729,167,590	516,110,067	3,082,841	13.9
Jalisco	6,989,085,747	1,325,430,530	8,348,151	45.7
México	7,404,950,849	5,750,450,827	16,992,418	39.3
Michoacán de Ocampo	883,903,290	771,957,051	4,748,846	10.5
Morelos	1,038,272,965	705,231,766	1,971,520	35.5
Nayarit	638,667,739	282,952,467	1,235,456	23.3
Nuevo León	4,877,817,303	3,035,936,560	5,784,442	18.1
Oaxaca	375,542,856	255,178,606	4,132,148	5.7
Puebla	1,231,291,240	915,333,908	6,583,278	9.5
Querétaro	4,996,556,682	2,136,204,742	2,368,467	7.9
Quintana Roo	2,467,310,916	1,677,135,586	1,857,985	37.0
San Luis Potosí	590,064,353	333,232,811	2,822,255	11.4
Sinaloa	2,008,164,196	1,430,938,251	3,026,943	17.9
Sonora	1,467,857,475	1,008,311,170	2,944,840	19.3
Tabasco	341,695,728	203,424,565	2,402,598	37.6
Tamaulipas	644,631,321	275,274,255	3,527,735	29.4
Tlaxcala	133,899,022	112,147,681	1,342,977	15.1
Veracruz de Ignacio de la Llave	1,262,921,955	777,623,446	8,062,579	35.6
Yucatán	1,182,353,993	644,107,056	2,320,393	13.7
Zacatecas	410,951,269	76,701,363	1,622,138	42.1

Censo de Población y Vivienda 2020
Conjunto de datos: Poblacióntotal. Liga: https://www.inegi.org.mx/sistemas/olap/consulta/general_ver4/MDXQueryDatos.asp?proy=
Sources: INEGI. Finanzaspúblicasestatales y municipales. Liga: https://www.inegi.org.mx/programas/finanzas/#Tabulados

values and to attract scarce labor and capital to its jurisdiction.[1] Weingast (2009) adds that this also fosters markets.[2]

Despite these benefits, Mexican recurrent property tax revenues are extremely low at 0.2% of GDP and have not surpassed 0.3% during the last 30 years. This is not just low among OECD countries (see Fig. 5.1 for a comparison with other federal OECD countries), but also within Latin America (Argentina: 0.4%; Brazil: 0.5%; Chile: 0.7% of GDP).[3]

Tax rates vary from one state to the next and from municipality to municipality. For example, a rate of 0.9 mills (0.09%) is applied on land and improvements in San Luis Potosi, 1.1 mills in Aguascalientes, 1.8 mills in Puebla, and 5 mills in Baja California. Of 32 federal entities, 21 apply a single rate, 9 apply progressive rates, and 2 progressive quotas for land value taxation. In the Federal District, a quota is applied, though efforts are being made to switch to a rent-based rate. Municipalities can suggest tax rates to the states, which then need to approve these through State Revenue Acts and State Tax Codes.

The tax base is the residential and commercial land and improvements (with some exceptions, notably Mexicali where only the land is taxed).

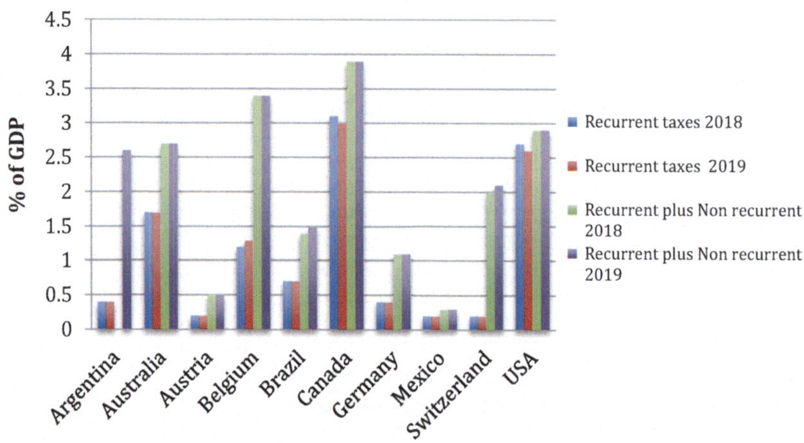

Fig. 5.1 Taxes on property in the federal OECD countries as percentage of GDP, 2018–9. (Source: OECD Revenue Statistics 2021. (Note: The data include all taxes on property, not only the property tax)

[1] See Tiebout (1956).

[2] See Weingast (2009).

[3] Peña Ahumada and Wence Partida (2011: 90).

The value of the land and improvements is determined in the cadaster and forms the base on which the tax rate is applied. The cadastral values assigned to land plots and buildings are used to determine the property tax, the tax on acquisitions of property, construction fees and licenses, tax on works contracts, on improvements of property, and so on, all of which correspond to tax powers of the municipality, according to Art 115 of the Constitution (since 1983). It is also used for other functions: it defines territorial limits, regulation of land ownership, environmental regulation, civil protection programs, and land value for expropriation. Together with the Public Registries of Property (RPP), it is also meant to provide legal certainty surrounding property rights; however, there are great discrepancies between the information contained in the cadasters and the RPPs causing legal uncertainty.

Who administers the cadasters? According to the constitution, the municipalities administer the cadaster. However, the constitution also provides the municipalities with the possibility of entering into agreements with the states in which the latter administer the tax in exchange for a commission. In recent years, an increasing number of municipalities have entered into such agreements and in around ten states decentralized "autonomous" cadastral institutes have been created, though few if any of these operate under complete (administrative, technical, legal, and financial) autonomy separate from the state.

2 Problems

A major obstacle to property tax revenues is outdated or flawed cadastral information. There are numerous "hidden" or omitted land plots and constructions that do not show up in the cadaster, largely because of a lack of updating. This is particularly relevant for sprawling urban municipalities that have experienced high levels of immigration. For example, a Banobras-led cadastral modernization program in Carmen, Campeche resulted in a rise of 54% in the number of land plots (from 53,713 to 82,890). Taxing these additional land plots that were formerly left out of the tax base is part of the reason for a rise of 120% in tax revenues from 25.8 million pesos in 2008 to 67.0 million pesos in 2011.[4] Very few municipalities have undergone such cadastral modernization programs to date.

Furthermore, cadastral values are far below market values, despite that the Constitution requires that they be comparable (Art 115 of the

[4] Data from Banobras (2012).

Constitution and Transitory Article V). Rough estimates of the discrepancy between cadastral values and market values have been made in 12 states. These vary greatly among states and among municipalities within the same states, with urban municipalities usually faring considerably better. On the high side, the equalization has reached up to 100% in Nayarit, 85–90% in the capital municipality of Aguascalientes (70% in its other municipalities), 80–85% in Estado de Mexico, and 80% in Guanajuato, while in others the figure is estimated to be far lower at 50% in Morelos and Tamaulipas, 40% in Colima, 30% in Oaxaca, and 10–20% in Tabasco. San Luis Potosi, Puebla, and Guerrero fall into a middle range at approximately 65% among the states that have produced such estimates.[5]

Another issue is that pending payments are not pursued, and non-compliance is not sanctioned. Estimates of the difference between registered property accounts and paid accounts have been conducted by a number of states, showing an average self-compliance rate of 71% (see Table 5.2). However, the reliability of these estimates appears suspect, particularly those that presume 100% compliance. Such data have been hard to come by and largely kept secretive as municipalities allegedly fear that if the extent of non-compliance is made public, even fewer people will pay the tax. Experts at Instituto para el Desarrollo Tecnico de las Haciendas Publicas (INDETEC) believe compliance to be closer to 50%. Using their estimates, there is a revenue potential of almost $8 billion pesos just from pursuing tax arrears (without updating cadastral information and values) (see Table 5.2).

Tax rates have remained static over time and, while generally low, represent less of a problem. More pernicious to revenues are the abundant exemptions and discounts. These differ from municipality to municipality, but usually include exemptions for historical patrimony, medical centers, ejidales, and communes, persons above the age of 60, handicapped persons, religious associations, charity organizations, and civil society associations as well as discounts for early payments. The largest exemption, however, secured in the constitution, is for government institutions and state-owned enterprises. All of these exemptions and special regimes cause revenue losses, inefficiencies and distortions and create opportunities for evasion. For example, municipal treasurers contend that a disproportionate number of properties are registered in the name of the elderly, that is, property purchases are placed in the name of elderly relatives.

[5] Data from INDETEC (2013).

Table 5.2 Level of compliance with the property tax as estimated by states, 2010

States	*Number of registered accounts*	*Number of accounts paid*	*Difference (paid minus unpaid accounts)*	*Level of compliance (number of accounts)*	*Level of compliance—INDETEC estimates*	*Level of lost revenues—INDETEC estimates*
Aguascalientes	464,333	349,701	114,632	75%	55%	56,075,858
Baja California	1,214,145	713,893	500,252	59%	19%	510,313,273
Baja California Sur	NA	NA	NA	NA	NA	NA
Campeche	259,135	125,446	133,689	48%	NA	NA
Coahuila	1,122,259	1,061,473	60,786	95%	38%	231,541,190
Colima	289,350	234,814	54,536	81%	28%	100,953,628
Chiapas	675,110	465,431	209,679	69%	52%	77,561,494
Chihuahua	1,260,756	743,984	516,772	59%	30%	600,936,411
Durango	767,012	378,652	388,360	49%	40%	82,318,123
Federal District	2,082,105	1,413,868	668,237	68%	69%	1,978,590,737
Guanajuato	1,609,442	1,474,426	135,016	92%	62%	329,125,733
Guerrero	NA	NA	NA	NA	NA	NA
Hidalgo	1,120,360	561,801	558,559	50%	37%	127,624,897
Jalisco	2,818,471	2,015,211	803,260	72%	35%	1,011,770,015
Mexico	NA	NA	NA	NA	72%	NA
Michoacan	1,416,107	1,176,049	240,058	83%	46%	227,682,765
Morelos	530,844	530,844	–	100%	51%	120,314,631
Nayarit	NA	NA	NA	NA	NA	NA
Nuevo Leon	1,786,241	989,673	796,568	55%	30%	800,963,142
Oaxaca	914,439	885,262	29,177	97%	49%	67,154,449
Puebla	1,852,186	616,312	1,235,874	33%	32%	261,823,961
Queretaro	568,852	443,035	125,817	78%	30%	323,339,551

(*continued*)

Table 5.2 (continued)

States	*Number of registered accounts*	*Number of accounts paid*	*Difference (paid minus unpaid accounts)*	*Level of compliance (number of accounts)*	*Level of compliance—INDETEC estimates*	*Level of lost revenues—INDETEC estimates*
Quintana Roo	456,258	396,620	59,638	87%	45%	427,281,033
San Luis Potosi	880,773	880,773	–	100%	31%	146,342,159
Sinaloa	947,861	947,861	–	100%	61%	249,343,736
Sonora	1,143,299	600,502	542,797	53%	77%	97,257,516
Tabasco	NA	NA	NA	NA	NA	NA
Tamaulipas	NA	NA	NA	NA	NA	NA
Tlaxcala	523,251	226,231	297,020	43%	91%	4,036,600
Veracruz	2,127,899	1,523,757	604,142	72%	NA	NA
Yucatan	634,128	512,177	121,951	81%	57%	88,712,431
Zacatecas	874,070	828,983	45,087	95%	67%	66,128,020
TOTAL	28,338,686	20,096,779	8,241,907	71%	48%	7,987,191,355

Source: Figures in black: Estimates reported by states; figures in blue: INDETEC

3 Causes of These Problems

The causes for these problems are to some extent administrative and financial, but essentially, they have to do with incentives. Focusing first on the administrative issues, managing a cadaster requires sophisticated tools, technology, and know-how. It requires a capable staff with regular and specialized training and processes that promote administrative efficiency and innovation. According to Morones Hernandez (2011), the current situation is one of generally poorly qualified staff, inadequate technology, and poor management systems.[6] Similarly, administering collection requires staff and resources.

There are numerous municipalities (particularly the small and urban) that do not have the technical or human capacity, nor the financial resources available for efficient cadastral management or collection. They are neither equipped to manage and update cadastral information nor to administer and pursue property tax payments. This leads to a situation in which over 520 municipalities (22%) collect no property tax at all.

3.1 Incentives

The property tax is politically unpopular because it is more visible than other taxes. The property tax is often used as a political tool. Granting exemptions is commonly used as concessions to pressure groups and promises to freeze the property tax is a frequent campaign pledge for winning elections. According to Morones Hernandez (2011, p. 121), "the property tax has become a political instrument more than an instrument to generate revenues."

In some instances, municipal governments want to raise revenues, but their efforts are disparaged by the state congress, which needs to approve any changes. The principal aim of state congress approval should be preventing ruthless over-collecting by the municipalities, but blocking of such efforts tends to be done for political reasons (such as sabotaging opposition party efforts) rather than for the protection of taxpayers. For example, in Aguascalientes, the legal basis for a cadastral modernization was only approved by the state once the party of the capital municipality became aligned with that of state, after at least eight years of failed attempts and delays. In La Paz, a municipal proposal to update tariffs was left

[6] Morones, Humberto (2012), July–Sept 2012, INDETEC, *Hacienda Municipal*, p. 84.

pending decision by the local congress from September 2011 for over a year until the municipality finally withdrew it. The proposal was simply left unattended to by the state. A resubmission the following year was finally blocked on no logical grounds. Similarly, interviews in Zapopan, Jalisco revealed that the local congress has regularly rejected requests to update the cadaster by certain opposition municipalities. Legal remedies to bypass ungrounded decisions or undue delays exist, but these are costly and rarely utilized.

Disincentives to collect the property tax are further abetted by the short-term periods of only three years with no consecutive reelection and a high staff turnover at the municipal level. The short-term periods promote short time horizons that discount the long-term in favor of more immediate payoffs. There is little incentive to implement a cadastral update since it involves a large upfront investment whose benefits only begin to be reaped in following years, once the government is no longer in power, that is, by its successors. One of the reasons cited why the municipality of Aguascalientes, Aguascalientes for deciding to pursue a cadastral modernization program was that the party in power (PRI) "very strong and had momentum" and predicted it would be reelected, as proved to be the case. It thus considered it viable to approve a cadaster modernization program at the start of its term. However, in many other cases, even if a cadastral modernization program is started, the project is often discontinued by the incoming local government due to a lack of continuity that an absence of a professionalized career civil service brings with it.

3.2 *Past Efforts and Their Shortcomings*

There have been continuous efforts at rectifying the issue of low property tax revenues over the past decades. Prior to a constitutional reform in 1983, the property tax was a state tax. Then municipalities were given the right to collect property taxes; however, states were left in charge of the cadasters. With no stake in the revenues, they had no incentive to update them. A further constitutional amendment to Article 115, which regulates municipal rights and obligations, in 1999 thus moved cadastral administration to the municipalities, with the option of entering into agreements with the states for the latter to administer the cadaster. They were also given the right to propose quotas and tariffs as well as the value tables that form the base of the tax, yet always with approval by the state congresses. To further address low property tax revenues, the constitutional amendment stipulated those cadastral values were to be comparable to market values. Despite these efforts, tax revenues failed to increase and cadastral values remain well below market values.

Changes to the transfer formulas have tried to work against the negative effect of increased fiscal transfers on municipal tax effort. As part of the 2007 fiscal reform, tax effort became a criterion in the transfer formula that distributes funds of the Fondo de Fomento Municipal to the states. The amount is a function of the annual rise in municipal revenues from the property tax and water fees in each state (but not of individual municipalities). Following Barry Weingast's 1/n law, if there are 30 municipalities in a state, for every peso a municipality generates, it will receive but 3 centavos. If there are 100 municipalities like Puebla, it will receive 1 centavo, thus providing only low marginal incentives to foster revenue collection (and leading to free riding of small municipalities on the efforts of the larger ones that can make more of difference).

However, in only six states (40% of municipalities) does the tax effort criterion predominate. In other states, it is rendered void or canceled out by other criteria. The Federal District, for example, made notable strides in improving property tax revenues, experiencing an 18.7% increase between 2010 and 2011 (and in improving revenues from water fees). However, given its decline in population over the same period, its rise in *participaciones* was miniscule.

Such economic incentives in the transfer formulas have been replicated at the state level in around 11 states to disburse funds between its municipalities. Again, they are ineffective as they may be canceled out by other criteria, such as population that render the tax effort criterion unimportant. According to Peña Ahumada and WencePartida (2011), in 2010 there were 12 states that used tax effort as a criterion for the *Fondo General de Participaciones*, but only 5 states did so in a clear, unequivocal manner that fosters tax effort, while in most other municipalities (90% of them), the transfer formulas were ambiguous.[7]

Various programs to modernize cadasters have been instigated over the past 30 years, including by federal institutions such as Secretaria de Desarrollo Social (SEDESOL), Instituto Nacional de Estadistica y Geografia (INEGI), and Banobras. Banobras created a special credit line as far back as 1987 to update cadasters.[8] In the early 1990s programs such as SEDESOL's Cadastral Modernization Program, and the Program of 100 Cities

[7] Peña Ahumado and Wence Partida (2011).

[8] Morones Hernandez (2011).

(Programa de 100 Ciudades) provided technical assistance and funding.[9] More recently in 2007, SEDESOL initiated a program with selected states to modernize their public property registries and cadasters (Programa de Modernizacion de los Registros Publicos de Propiedad y Catastros). This program has the primary objective of integrating cadastral information and the information contained in the public registries of property (RPP) into a single database in order to improve legal certainty and security of property rights. It also advises setting up an autonomous institution in each state to link these as well as introducing tools to improve information systems, service efficiency and professionalization of cadastral functions. To date, three "model" states have entered the program (Campeche, Morelos, and Colima).

Banobras, together with INEGI, has continued its cadastral modernization programs in which they support municipalities with technical support (including an initial diagnosis, recommendations, and evaluation) and finally reimburses municipalities with between 40% and 50% of the costs of the cadastral modernization. The first 14 municipalities that completed the program experienced a 15% increase in the number of registered property accounts and a 52% increase in collection, with a further rise expected in coming years given that ceilings tend to be imposed for year on year rises in the tax.[10] This shows the potential of widening the tax base alone.

These programs are on the right track, but experience many of the problems outlined above. The SEDESOL program has been criticized for not tying cadastral updates to tax collection. Municipal leaders do not use the updated information to also update the basis for tax payments. For instance, the Banobras program is designed to take between 8 and 14 months, but many municipalities experience delays or discontinue efforts. One hundred fourteen municipalities were invited to the program since 2006. Of these only 75 decided to be incorporated into the program and only 17 have completed the program (58 are advancing with delays). Among the reasons cited are a lack of funds and changes in political agendas after a change in government; a general lack of political will on the part of the municipal leaders is evident.

[9] See Banobras (1997).

[10] Data from Banobras December 2012.

4 Options for Reform

4.1 Reduce Reliance of Municipalities on Bailouts

Reliance on higher-level rescues and amnesties is a moral hazard that has contributed to a neglect of own revenues. The absence of adequate own-source revenues under the control of states and metro areas/cities reduces the sustainable access to credit or direct borrowing, issuance of bonds, or PPPs.

4.2 De-politicize Collection: Administration and Auditing by SAT or Independent Agency

The political resistance to raising property taxes arises from their visibility and how they are administered. It is a periodic lump-sum payment paid directly to the municipality. Having a different institution collect the tax and sanction non-compliance will take political pressure off of the municipality, especially temptations to pardon increases and create exemptions. The taxpayers are far more aware of any increase in the tax bill (even if just nominal increases to maintain real revenues) than with taxes that are, say, added on to the price of a good or automatically deduced from their take-home salary. Furthermore, taxpayers easily link the quantity and quality of local services to tax payments. They are particularly quick to question a rise in the taxes if services have not improved.

A solution is to have an institution different from the municipality administer tax collection. One option is to have the SAT administer and audit property taxes. A substantial increase of total collections would be a pre-requisite to maintain incentives to SAT. Alternatively, independent agencies could be set up to administer local taxes and sanction non-payment.

The downside of moving collection and audit to a separate institution is that it would make the property tax less visibly a municipal tax, thus weakening the (potential) accountability mechanism linking local taxes to local services. However, this can be maintained by giving municipal governments power over the tax rate (see below).

4.3 *Allow Municipalities to Set the Rate Without Approval of the State Legislature*

Currently municipal decisions to change the tax rate require approval by the state congress. This approval requirement was implemented to prevent municipal governments from drastically raising taxes but this fear has proven unwarranted. Also, through electoral accountability, municipal governments in any case fear the political costs associated with raising the tax rate.

The most important characteristic of a local tax (what makes a tax a local tax) is the ability of the local government to determine the tax rate.[11] Not allowing the municipal government to set the tax rate precludes the mechanisms that make the local government be accountable to its constituents at the margin, as both democracy and efficiency require.

4.4 *Economic Incentives Through Improved Transfer Formulas*

Reliance on increased transfers also vilifies tax effort. The negative consequences of transfers (especially earmarked) on fiscal responsibility and tax effort have been documented elsewhere (see Raich Portman 2004; Cabrero 2006: 3). To be sure, transfers are necessary as own revenues do not suffice even to cover current expenditures in most municipalities. However, making transfers from higher levels of government dependent on the tax effort can counteract against these perverse incentives. These need to be designed in a way that the gain is obvious and substantial to the municipalities. This implies that each municipality's tax effort should count, not simply the state aggregate, otherwise the incentive applies only to the large municipalities while the small municipalities free riding on their efforts. The proportionate gain in transfers from revenues also needs to be made more explicit. For example, if municipalities were to receive, for example, double of what they earned in revenue in addition to other shared revenues, this would make the gain far more clear and incite action than making it as only one of the various other criteria in a complicated transfer formula.

[11] Bird (1999).

5 Toward a Beneficial Property Tax in Mexico

Apart from the poor connectivity, one of the main constraints in getting firms to locate in say Chiapas or Oaxaca in the Southern part of Mexico is the low levels of local services and amenities. This also limits the attractiveness of these states for higher qualified workers, often needed for the requisite private investments to be undertaken. Simple metrics of migration can be misleading, as we saw above, there has been reverse migration of workers returning to their extended support networks from the informal sector, for example, in CDMX and Veracruz, given the economic crises during the past decade.

An agenda for sustained recovery from the pandemic, addressing long-term trade and environmental shocks must involve a local tax system that:

- Can be implemented quickly,
- Is able to generate a sufficient level of revenues to finance basic health spending at the minimum, plus other local services,
- Should be attractive distributionally,
- Facilitates local accountability, and
- Helps with the spatial dynamics of urban transformation—that is, the tax in Chiapas must be significantly lower than say in CDMX or Club 1 states, to generate the right incentives for firms and workers.

As in the Chinese case illustrated above, Ahmad and Viscarra (2020[12]) simulate the effects of a recurrent property tax on non-business properties that is based on simple measures of location and size and calibrated to cover basic public services (proxied in this case by spending on education). Given that there is generally an active market for business properties, it is desirable to maintain the valuation-ownership property tax model for such properties (this is also the case in the UK and in China).

A very simple method is used where the tax is determined according to a tax rate applied to the size and location of the property. The rate per square meter is set in relation to the built-up areas, and a broad indicator of level of development, proxied in this example by State level GDP. In practice, an average rate/square meter for a state will probably be too low

[12] Ahmad, E. and H. Viscarra (2020), "Financing Clean, Compact and Connected Cities in Mexico: role of a "beneficial" property tax," *LSE Program on Sustainable Transitions in China and Mexico.*

for some cities (and localities within cities) and too high for others, but is being used for purely illustrative purposes, pending more detailed city-level assessments that might follow at a later stage. This method sidesteps problems with complicated cadasters (that are still needed for legal purposes and for business properties), ownership, and valuation complications, and can be implemented relatively quickly.

Table 5.3 illustrates the method. The simple beneficial property tax is seen to be highly differentiated and is likely to play a very strong role in the spatial dynamics of urban transformation in Mexico. The tax rate/m^2 is set at 1.5% of State GDP and varies from Mx\$437/m^2 in CDMX to Mx\$88/m^2 in Chiapas.

The distributional consequences of the beneficial property tax in Mexico are striking. The inequality effect is calculated for low, medium, and higher levels of inequality aversion ($e = 0.5$, 1, and 2), and compares the original level of inequality without tax, Y_0, Y_1 the tax on its own, and Y_2 with the tax distributed equally, or to families with children for education/health spending. As seen in Table 5.4, the tax on its own reduces inequality in most states—this is seen most markedly for Chiapas, and the effect is magnified as the benefit linkages are introduced, and inequality aversion increased. Given the importance of the poor in Chiapas, this is a very powerful result.

The CDMX case is of interest. The tax on its own leads to increased inequality at low levels of inequality aversion. However, the situation changes when linked to benefits targeted to children—in this case for education. But if there are moderate or high levels of inequality aversion, the tax on its own reduces inequality in CDMX, and the impact of linkage with either equal distribution of benefits, or targeted to education is even stronger. Clearly, the tax-benefit linkage is a very powerful policy tool for a government that is very concerned with inequality and creating sustainable employment hubs, especially in the lagging southern states of the country.

Relative to the current collection of 0.26% of GDP on account of the property tax, the proposed 1.5% of State revenues on average would give a tremendous revenue boost to the own-source revenue potential in every state. This would open the doors to a more systematic use of private finance for public infrastructure, including green bonds, without exacerbating risks from sub-national liabilities.

The most significant increases in revenue potential are in CDMX as well as in Chiapas. This makes the reform of interest in both rich and poorer

Table 5.3 Determining the rate of a beneficial property tax in Mexico Mx$/m^2. Source: Ahmad and Viscarra (2020)

States	*Average property size (m²)*	*Expected income 1.5% of GDP (millions of pesos)*	*Tax MX$/square meter*
AgCal	95.3	2.973	180.73
Baja Calif.	83.5	7.589	201.45
Baja Calif. S	72.8	1.951	245.71
Campeche	75.3	1.904	190.38
Coahuila	98.2	8.608	210.17
Colima	88.6	1.430	186.38
Chiapas	64.5	4.357	87.88
Chihuahua	102.2	7.728	190.04
CDMX	92.2	42.548	437.87
Durango	96.6	2.925	122.18
Guanajuato	96.2	9.918	134.79
Guerrero	61.9	3.480	109.61
Hidalgo	80.3	3.804	108.19
Jalisco	99.6	16.615	178.73
Mexico	77.8	21.578	115.45
Michoacan	77.7	5.875	122.13
Morelos	79.3	2.797	141.74
Nayarit	89.1	1.723	110.34
Nuevo L.	93.1	18.289	264.25
Oaxaca	64.8	3.908	98.60
Puebla	77.9	8.092	123.49
Queretaro	88.8	5.548	211.16
Quintana R	69.6	3.683	255.96
Potosí	94.6	4.952	126.40
Sinaloa	72.0	5.429	161.94
Sonora	85.4	8.062	215.33
Tabasco	76.9	3.935	138.19
Tamaulipas	82.3	7.359	227.69
Tlaxcala	79.3	1.449	97.65
Veracruz	72.4	12.060	139.58
Yucatan	73.5	3.483	152.41
Zacatecas	93.1	2.388	133.93

Source: INEGI and Ahmad and Viscarra (2020)

states. However, the tax potential in CDMX is almost ten times the revenues that could accrue to Chiapas (Table 5.4) and twice the revenue potential of the measure in the State of Mexico (the next highest). In

Table 5.4 Mexican states: initial distribution of income Y_0 and distributional impact of area-based property tax Y_1, and links to basic services Y_2 for different levels of inequality aversion

	e = 0.5				*e = 1*				*e = 2*			
	Y0	*Y1*	*Y2*	*Y2*	*Y0*	*Y1*	*Y2*	*Y2*	*Y0*	*Y1*	*Y2*	*Y2*
Estados		*(Y0-property tax 1,5% PIB)*	*(target)*	*(equal)*		*(Y0-property tax 1,5% PIB*	*(target)*	*(equal)*		*(Y0-property tax 1,5% PIB)*	*(target)*	*(equal)*
Aguas Calientes	0.152	0.160	0.09	0.134	0.297	0.308	0.176	0.261	0.541	0.55	0.338	0.477
Baja California	0.204	0.215	0.154	0.188	0.353	0.373	0.255	0.325	0.574	0.598	0.375	0.515
Baja California Sur	0.185	0.219	0.132	0.208	0.331	0.382	0.244	0.367	0.539	0.59	0.42	0.576
Campeche	0.271	0.219	0.085	0.166	0.431	0.379	0.158	0.289	0.618	0.585	0.281	0.458
Coahuila	0.186	0.135	0.066	0.121	0.334	0.264	0.125	0.242	0.555	0.484	0.225	0.464
Colima	0.167	0.172	0.081	0.148	0.304	0.313	0.154	0.269	0.519	0.52	0.282	0.448
Chiapas	0.436	0.246	0.08	0.14	0.620	0.450	0.155	0.261	0.807	0.72	0.287	0.456
Chihuahua	0.195	0.158	0.078	0.133	0.351	0.301	0.142	0.250	0.569	0.531	0.241	0.437
CDMX	0.148	0.151	0.144	0.151	0.278	0.277	0.263	0.275	0.496	0.467	0.436	0.461
Durango	0.172	0.166	0.063	0.129	0.316	0.322	0.125	0.252	0.541	0.584	0.244	0.464
Guanajuato	0.168	0.154	0.091	0.116	0.317	0.289	0.162	0.219	0.569	0.517	0.271	0.395
Guerrero	0.206	0.177	0.068	0.131	0.385	0.354	0.130	0.262	0.634	0.634	0.234	0.485
Hidalgo	0.239	0.283	0.099	0.203	0.426	0.490	0.172	0.346	0.683	0.761	0.278	0.528
Jalisco	0.170	0.172	0.141	0.144	0.314	0.315	0.248	0.265	0.553	0.554	0.395	0.469
Mexico	0.191	0.182	0.157	0.139	0.354	0.344	0.289	0.265	0.599	0.604	0.48	0.476
Michoacan	0.228	0.226	0.109	0.171	0.404	0.404	0.192	0.309	0.642	0.635	0.308	0.508

Morelos	0.222	0.254	0.132	0.206	0.387	0.456	0.234	0.369	0.615	0.717	0.379	0.594
Nayarit	0.201	0.221	0.113	0.186	0.366	0.403	0.215	0.340	0.619	0.684	0.417	0.597
Nuevo Leon	0.162	0.154	0.126	0.139	0.295	0.284	0.226	0.257	0.494	0.475	0.362	0.442
Oaxaca	0.230	0.221	0.089	0.158	0.428	0.421	0.178	0.307	0.703	0.723	0.364	0.573
Puebla	0.285	0.225	0.121	0.171	0.461	0.403	0.211	0.312	0.688	0.656	0.336	0.527
Queretaro	0.199	0.203	0.104	0.166	0.363	0.374	0.193	0.307	0.627	0.657	0.35	0.546
Quintana Roo	0.149	0.149	0.07	0.132	0.286	0.278	0.138	0.250	0.525	0.472	0.269	0.441
Potosí	0.274	0.247	0.13	0.205	0.486	0.449	0.230	0.370	0.748	0.72	0.378	0.602
Sinaloa	0.175	0.188	0.075	0.155	0.335	0.351	0.140	0.292	0.585	0.585	0.246	0.494
Sonora	0.190	0.188	0.12	0.168	0.331	0.327	0.202	0.293	0.536	0.536	0.311	0.48
Tabasco	0.213	0.206	0.106	0.172	0.392	0.391	0.206	0.333	0.654	0.677	0.407	0.607
Tamaulipas	0.190	0.191	0.122	0.168	0.346	0.354	0.222	0.311	0.584	0.59	0.363	0.517
Tlaxcala	0.184	0.182	0.084	0.134	0.340	0.349	0.166	0.256	0.597	0.643	0.323	0.466
Veracruz	0.248	0.217	0.152	0.174	0.423	0.390	0.259	0.315	0.659	0.648	0.399	0.528
Yucatan	0.237	0.241	0.106	0.191	0.415	0.422	0.189	0.338	0.658	0.65	0.31	0.531
Zacatecas	0.309	0.212	0.077	0.154	0.470	0.369	0.152	0.276	0.655	0.613	0.309	0.48

Source: Ahmad and Viscarra (2020)

order to prevent the measure from increasing spatial inequality and reversing the dynamics of urban transformation, it is important to pose the reforms jointly with a modern fiscal equalization reworking of the *participaciones*, as recommended in Ahmad et al. (2007).[13]

6 Some Lessons from the Sub-national Tax Reform Agenda

Sub-national own-source taxes, where a jurisdiction has control over rates at the margin, are critical in the recovery from the pandemic and sustainable growth agenda. Not only do they provide additional revenues for basic expenditures, such as on preventive health care and services such as clean water and sanitation, they provide incentives for firms and workers, as well as governments at different levels to engage in more sustainable activities, and to reduce informality.

The own-source revenues can also open up the critical area of private sector financing, by determining a "sustainable level" of access to borrowing (of all kinds). But it is important to include all liabilities on the balance sheets of the relevant government, as emphasized in the previous section. As the experience from the 1990s road building program reminds Mexican policy makers, project-related bonds even without public guarantees can become budgetary liabilities at times of stress—usually through non-performing loans in the banking system.

Finally, even when well designed, such as the beneficial property tax, it is important to keep the overall policy framework in mind, particularly the issue of spatial dynamics of urban transitions. Thus, in isolation, the beneficial property tax would probably increase spatial inequalities, as the divergence between the clubs, particularly the two outliers at either end—CDMX and Chiapas—grows even larger. For this, we turn to the last set of instruments that must be kept in mind in devising a successful and sustainable growth trajectory.

6.1 *The Role of Fiscal Equalization in the Sustainable Employment Generation Agenda*

The growing spatial imbalances have been a central part of the policy dialogue in Mexico for well over two decades. Addressing such inequalities is

[13] Ahmad et al. (2007).

sensibly at the heart of the economic program of the current administration. The pandemic adds further urgency to the challenges faced, given that the poor are likely to face a disproportionately high burden of adjustment. This will have implications for metropolitan areas, such as CDMX that have the highest infection and mortality rates, but there could be a lagged effect of reverse migration to the lagging regions such as Chiapas, especially if the coping mechanisms adopted in the past decade come into play. In addition to the tax instruments, discussed above, that directly influence income distribution, it is useful to distinguish between the two other instruments available—current and capital transfers/public investments.

In Latin American countries, equalization in practice is often based on closing actual gaps in poverty levels or public services and providing financing accordingly. Although this appears appealing, the analytical framework is similar to that of means tested transfers, which also underpinned the *Oportunidades/Progresa* program. But as the recipients in an equalization program are sub-national governments, the disincentive effects of current equalization practices are quite pronounced. If actual gaps, such as in specific services and poverty levels are incorporated into policy design, it is in the interest of the recipient administration to maximize the gaps, and not close them. Similarly, if actual revenues are used (even if a fiscal effort measure is included), the recipient government would not be inclined to increase own-source revenues. This is consistent with the poor state of sub-national revenue performance in Mexico and many other Latin American countries. The incentive structure thus becomes perverse and is likely to result in "good intentions, bad outcomes."

In a major component of the research program, Ahmad and Viscarra (2020) estimate for Mexico a fiscal equalization model adapted from best practice, in many OECD countries as well as China. This looks at standardized disabilities faced by specific jurisdictions with respect to key spending functions. Thus, high costs of education provision might arise due to population density in metropolitan areas, as well as in dispersed populations requiring special instruction in say Chiapas. The standardized spending differentials are combined with the differentials in relation to revenue generation. The standardized differentials are linked to independent factors not under the control of the sub-national jurisdiction. The composite disability becomes the basis for an effective "lump sum" transfer that can be juxtaposed against the current system of untied transfers

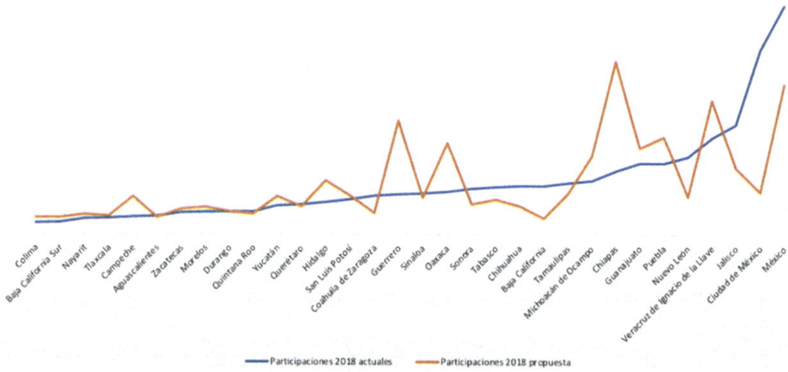

Fig. 5.2 Need to supplement a system of own-source revenues with an equalization system—reworking the 2018 *participaciones* (Ahmad and Viscarra 2020)

(*participaciones*). The details of models and estimations are provided in Ahmad and Viscarra (2020).

Figure 5.2 summarizes the findings and suggests a need to vary the *participaciones* so that the system is closer effective fiscal equalization—permitting different governments to provide similar levels of service at similar levels of tax effort. Again, the contrasts between the two outliers—CDMX and Chiapas—are interesting. CDMX, which has the highest income levels, also has one of the highest *participaciones* transfers. An equalization system would give Chiapas the highest level of transfers, whereas that for CDMX would be reduced. However, given the disabilities of expenditure needs in congested metropolitan areas, the CDMX transfer would still be higher than rich states like Baja California or Nuevo León, or the southern state of Quintana Roo (which has excellent services). This result reinforces that from Ahmad et al. (2007), which focused mainly on spending needs.

The basis for capital transfers or investments should be driven by a proper shadow pricing exercise and assessment of sustainable urban dynamics for the building better exercise, as discussed above.

References

Ahmad E, Gonzalez Anaya J, Brosio G, García-Escribano M, Lockwood B, and Revilla E., (2007) Why Focus on Spending Needs Factors? The Political Economy of Fiscal Transfer Reforms in Mexico. IMF Working Papers.

Ahmad, E. and H. Viscarra (2020), "Financing Clean, Compact and Connected Cities in Mexico: role of a "beneficial" property tax," LSE Program on Sustainable Transitions in China and Mexico.

Banobras (1997) La ModernizacionCatastral en elPrograma de 100 Ciudades. RevistaFederalismo y Desarrollo. No. 58

Banobras (2012), Excel Data Sheet, *Banco Nacional de Obras y Servicios Publicos.*

Bird R., (1999) Threading the Fiscal Labyrinth: Some Issues in Fiscal Decentralization. In Slemdod, Joel (ed) Tax Policy in the Real World. Cambridge University Press, New York.

Cabrero Mendoza, Enrique (2006) "Los Retos Institucionales de la descentralizacion fiscal en America Latina", CIDE, division de Administración Pública Documento de Trabajo, No 181.

INDETEC (2013) Revista Hacienda Municipal.

Morones Hernandez, Humberto (2011) "Aumentar la Recaudacion Predial: reto de la Hacienda Municipal" Revista Hacienda Municipal, July-Sept, 2011: p.121.

Morones Hernandez, Humberto (2012), "Por que los Avances en la Modernizacion Catastral no se han Traducido en una Exitosa Recaudacion Predial". July-Sept 2012.

Peña Ahumada and Wence Partida, (2011). "La Distribución de Transferencias Federales para Municipios", Revista Hacienda Municipal, Oct-Dec.: p.90.

Raich Portman, Uri (2004) "Impacto de la descentralización del gasto en los municipios mexicanos", CIDE, Division de Economia, Documento de trabajo No.281.

Tiebout C., (1956). A Pure Theory of Local Expenditures, Journal of Political Economy, University of Chicago Press, vol. 64, pages 416.

Weingast B., (2009) Second Generation of Fiscal Federalism: The implications of fiscal incentives". Journal of Urban Economics. 65, (3) :279-293.

CHAPTER 6

Administration of Property Taxes

Abstract In keeping with trends in modern tax administration, the colonial tax administrator model should be replaced by a functional structure of the administration to minimize contacts with taxpayers and limit rent-seeking and corruption opportunities. The area-based model with a focus on occupancy is much easier to administer than the value-based model, although a cadaster might still be needed for legal purposes and for business properties. High-tech satellite imagery, with low-tech verification show promise even in less developed countries, and blockchain would make a big difference in recording transactions, revenues generated as well as enhancing local public financial management options. Blockchain creates an immutable public registry not under control of any single agent, and is a powerful instrument for improving the management of data in the public sector, and also for registering property ownership and sales.

Keywords Functional tax administration • Cadasters and registers • Digital platforms and blockchains

Administrative constraints at the local level are often blamed for the poor performance of the property tax in many developing countries. Complexities associated with identifying and registering properties often create opportunities for rent-seeking and taxpayers often pay a great deal

E. Ahmad, G. Brosio, *Beneficial Property Taxation for Emerging Market Countries*, https://doi.org/10.1007/978-3-031-08612-0_6

more than the amounts collected in the national or local treasuries. The simplicity of an area-based tax and the use of modern technology such as satellite imagery and blockchain can considerably reduce rent-seeking and corruption. The key element in accountability is the ability of the local government to set rates (perhaps within a band set at the state or national level, depending on the constitutional arrangements). It does not matter if the key elements of a functional administration are not local, as long as the monies collected are deposited promptly and fully in the accounts of the local administration.

We argue that strengthened reliance on the colonial "tax collector" model can be counterproductive; that a modern functional administration is necessary for arm's length operations that do not have to be local; and that new technologies like satellite imagery and blockchain options can simplify and reduce opportunities for corruption while simplifying both the revenue and treasury circuits. Countries from India to Tanzania and Mexico have been seeking to put some distance between the tax collection process and the taxpayer. This is part of a move to address rampant corruption. We outline some options in this chapter.

1 Limits of Colonial "Tax Collector" Administration

The typical colonial model for the administration of the property tax outside cities was an important functionary called the "tax collector." This functionary was often from an elite administrative service; played a dual role with local administration; and formed an interface between the colonial masters and the native people of the colonies. Post-independence, the colonial oversight disappeared, and local governments lacked incentives to effectively manage the "collectors." Proximity to taxpayers opened avenues for rent-seeking and failed to generate any significant public revenues.

Proposals to use incentive payments for the tax collectors merely reinforce a colonial administrative structure. However, while the experiments show that some improvements are possible in the experimental sites, it is not clear that the results from experiments in Pakistan can be generalized, as the country's tax collections remain dismal, and the perception remains that the local tax administration is a cesspool of corruption. The principal difficulty with the method is that it continues to encourage direct contact between the taxpayers and the revenue collector—the old colonial model in South Asia worked when the collector was a well-paid British official but breaks down with local officials who can make deals with friends and relatives. Besides, this is the antithesis of modern administration, in which a functional structure is used, and no single administrator or function can take credit for revenue performance, but it is efficiency of the whole system that matters (see below and Ahmad 2015).

2 Viable Approaches for Emerging and Developing Countries

2.1 *Self-Assessment Together with a Modern Tax Administration*

A self-assessment system may generate a substantial and sustained increase in property tax revenues, and obviate temporarily to deficiencies of cadaster and valuation, as experimented in Bogotá by Mayor Mockus in 1994 when attempted to expand property tax collections (also see below). The cadaster and valuation basis were retained as a minimum.[1] It relied on the sanction of forcible purchase of the property at a multiple of the declared value in egregious cases of under-declaration of property values. There is no need for a heavy-handed use of the sanction, and one or two examples suffice. However, there is the danger that the sanctions might be used for "political" purposes, although the Bogotá system is still in operation despite changes in city administrations.

A true self-assessment system requires an arm's length trust system, with a high probability of detection, relatively good information on local property tax transactions, and credible sanctions. These are all characteristics of a modern functional tax administration—which we examine in the next section.

There is very limited cross-country information on administrative costs for property taxes, and much depends on how the tax is designed and the administration model used. Indeed, the case-by-case information on the

[1] Colombia has now a reasonably good system of property records and cadaster, based on an independent and arms-length agency: *Instituto Geográfico Augustín*, established in 1935, and now under the Statistics agency. Its responsibilities include the management of official maps and basic cartography and soil surveys, as well as the cadaster. The basic problem remains that the valuations are not particularly up to date or accurate, and the tax collections were low.

administrative arrangements is even more patchy than the revenue collection data. Bird (2011) argues that land and property taxes are "surprisingly costly," but the surprise factor disappears after considering the complexity of levying a property tax according to the traditional approach based on fully fledged cadaster and assessment of value of each individual property. Furthermore, evaluation of the cost issue has to include the benefits of property taxation (both individual and collective) that are much more relevant than with other taxes.

We have to distinguish between fixed costs, like setting up a land registry or cadaster, and recurrent costs, which are defined by the costs of assessing land value and collecting taxes, and which are dominated by costs of assessors and employees in the tax administration. Very often, the skilled personnel needed, such as surveyors to estimate the separate property improvement in Tanzania, were just not available.

There are no comprehensive assessments of fixed costs of property taxes. The limited available evidence (Kalkuhl et al., 2017) derives mostly from World Bank and other donors' projects for creating land registries. According to this source, set-up costs range typically between US$10 and $100 million. A project for the creation of a land registry in Ghana, for example, cost about $55 m (approx. 0.1% of GDP) and another in Laos was about $28 m (approx. 1% of GDP). A World Bank project on the long-term development of Indonesia's institutional capacity for land administration had an up-front cost of $140 m (approx. 0.1% of GDP). There are, however, substantial chances that these figures provide an underassessment of costs since in many cases projects remain largely incomplete, and there are no incentives to recognize the full costs, especially if some are borne by other levels of government, as discussed below. The field visits to Senegal and Tanzania also confirm that, despite a decades-long process, the building of cadaster still has a long way to go in both countries. This likely applies also (as the team was informed) to a World Bank project on *adressage* in Dakar with a cost of $50 m. Indeed, in Senegal the bulk of the costs of administering the property tax is borne by the Treasury.

Only a few studies exist that quantify full administration costs. Very interestingly, Blažić et al. (2014) estimate that in Croatia, administration costs as a percentage of property tax collections vary enormously, between 5% and 50%. Higher costs are usually paid by smaller municipalities that can rely less on economies of scale in assessing property values. A comprehensive study on property taxes in Latin American municipalities (De

Cesare 2016) reveals substantially lower costs of 1–20% of total taxes raised, with 6% costs for a median municipality. The large variability of administrative costs suggests that there is substantial potential for cost reduction with the adoption of flat taxes. Also, important scale economies exist as shown by the experience of Croatia, and these can be exploited with centralization of property tax administration. This would also have an impact by equalizing the costs of administration across the whole country, to the benefit of the poorer regions.

With a functional model, the synergies between the property tax and a national income tax can be better harnessed, with a central enforcement function. This includes both the data warehouse and exchange of information across tax heads, as well as critical audit functions that are hard to manage at the local level. Similarly, the use of modern technology, including satellite imagery may make more sense if managed at the national level.

The blockchain options represent a radical departure in that local information is generated at relatively low cost. However, this has major implications on the processes and procedures linked to the tax administration as well as cash-management/treasury functions that can be greatly simplified, and overall functioning costs of both the tax and PFM systems reduced accordingly. However, there will be a greater need to ensure proper overall management and audit—and this again will reinforce a national functional system to support the new technology. This is a major area of work, as it offers greater accuracy and potential savings on overall tax and treasury functions, even though higher costs of audit and some technological elements may also have to be factored in.

3 Tax Administration Options for Arms' Length Operation of Local Taxes

A functional model delineates rate setting and the administrative functions and provides for an arms' length basis for managing several taxes together.

An own-source revenue is one where the jurisdiction controls rate setting at the margin (e.g., within a band). This applies even if all the elements of administration are handled by another jurisdiction or an independent agency (Ahmad 2015). Conversely, even if a local authority controls all elements of the administration, but is unable to control the rate, the resulting revenue is not own-source, in the sense that it cannot be increased to say meet additional financing needs. Similarly, shared revenues are not own-source and are similar to intergovernmental transfers (e.g., through an equalization framework where the local jurisdiction has no ability to influence the allocations). The own-source revenues are critical for the local accountability that is needed for a successful decentralization program.

It is common in modern tax administrations to have different functional specializations. These include registration, valuation, assessments, bill delivery, collection, enforcement,[2] and taxpayer services. Many of these functions operate across taxes, facilitate the exchange of information across tax instruments, and prevent the duplication of similar operations. The most egregious example of duplication of functions is the operation of the Tanzanian land tax and property tax, with different agencies carrying out the same function (see below).

Under a functional structure, the total revenue collection is the result of all the components acting in coordination, and not one person operating independently. Consequently, it is difficult to ascribe the additionality in revenues to any one individual, and it is hard to introduce an individual performance-based criterion in relation to revenue generation.

Not all the functions need to be carried out in the same agency. It is typical for the property tax to have a separate body responsible for the cadaster, as this also has legal implications regarding ownership. The formal rural-urban distinction is not particularly useful if "urban" is strictly defined as falling within municipal boundaries, as a great deal of construction takes place in adjacent territories that are de facto part of the urban areas, but are classified as rural (e.g., settlements around Cairo).

3.1 *Registration*

For the purposes of registering a property tax, it is important to identify where the properties are located, more or less in real time. This may not be possible with the cadaster that takes a considerable time to update. The most practical option for most emerging market economies would be to focus on occupancy for the property tax. In situations where the ownership is hard to disentangle, this is possibly the only feasible option. This can be achieved with several alternatives or combinations of options:

[2] Note: Enforcement would include both (1) the maintenance of a common database on transactions and assets, using tax and third party information, and (2) audit. Source: Ahmad (2015).

- *Using the principle of self-declaration* that underlies modern tax administration requires occupants to register with local governments or other responsible administration. This could be linked to the right to vote, and access to public services, including health clinics and public schools. It should also be linked to access to credit, and if a national identification number has been established (see, e.g., the Pakistani electronically maintained database for the National Identity Card (NIC) using biometrics being replicated in Nigeria). The Bogotá experience with self-declarations subject to selective audit and sanctions (that included resumption/purchase of the property at above the declared value) worked both vis-à-vis identifying properties that were not yet in the cadaster (supposedly one of the best in Latin America), but also identification of market value (more on valuation below)—although this is not strictly needed in the simple area-based systems that may be relevant for emerging markets (adaptation of the UK model).

  In agricultural areas, with the ownership largely vested in the state or traditional property rights, it might be useful to register tenancy or use-contracts. This provides a degree of protection to the tenant to be able to make investments on the land and to access credit. As proposed in Ahmad and Stern (1991) for South Asia, it might be useful to make a distinction between rain-fed and irrigated lands, and to exclude the smallest operational holdings from the payment of the tax—but they must be registered to receive the benefits of secure tenancy and access to credit.
- *Using satellite imagery*: as in Mwanza and other cities in Tanzania, this can provide very accurate delineations of properties and their size. This can be achieved quickly, together with the identification of the number of inhabitants, which can be established through self-declaration, as well as through verification by survey teams.

  Many local mapping projects exist—from private citizens mapping their local *neighborhoods* to larger efforts concerning disaster relief or food safety. A successful example from Tanzania is a mapping effort in Dar es Salaam (http://ramanihuria.org/). Originally created to assess flooding risks, this group has trained more than 400 volunteers and has provided a detailed map of Dar es Salaam, including its informal settlements. It uses satellite imagery combined with images taken by drones to create very detailed maps (see Fig. 6.1).

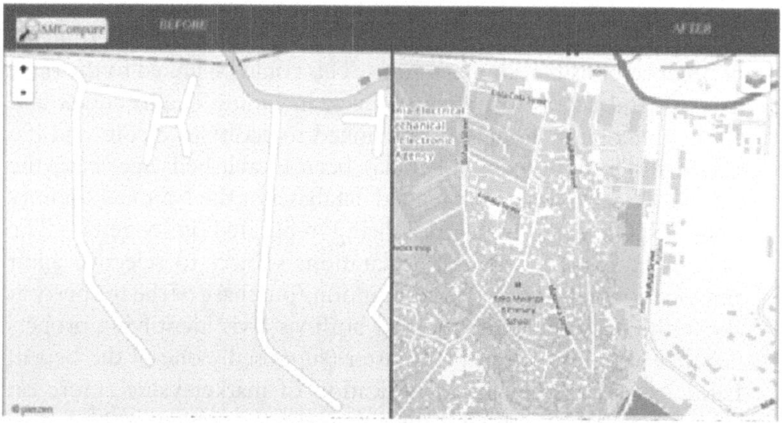

Fig. 6.1 OSM in Dar es Salaam, before and after satellite imagery

Open Streep Map (OSM) (https://www.openstreetmap.org) is an international collaborative mapping project where all data is freely available and reusable. One way to describe it is "the Wikipedia of Google maps." Importantly, Open Street Map is not just a data standard for data: it is an ecosystem of users and developers, which have created tools to edit and visualize these data. This is a process of creating crowd-sourced maps through "interactive community mapping". The fact that OSM data are open and free to re-use and extend upon, makes it an interesting project to build upon for many different organizations and purposes. In practice, this means that there are people present with knowledge and competence of mapping technology and the associated software that may (and probably should) be leveraged.

While publishing cadastral data in OSM is clearly recommendable, it may also be used to create and expand on cadastral maps. Of interest is *Cadasta* (cadasta.org), an open-source software framework specifically created to address the creation of land registers in developing countries.

3.2 *Valuation*

The traditional argument for valuation to be local is that there is generally good local information on property transactions. While this used to be true in the past, modern internet-based generation of information, and tools such as Zillow, allow governments and the public anywhere seeking information on property values in the US, or around the world, for example, to be able to track property sales and resulting market values in US states.

The local information base is more limited in emerging market economies, which is why the valuation-based models tend not to work (in many countries, e.g., in South Asia, the true values are typically not declared). However, developments in technology, better recording of property transactions, and modern administration mechanisms can make a significant difference. Use of area-based taxes allows local governments to overcome the valuation problem, until capacity is developed to make use of the best developments in technology.

3.3 Collection

Under a traditional model of administration, local officials are responsible for collections, as well as exemptions. This has the advantage of local information available to the officials that can be used to ensure that the correct amounts are collected, and can potentially enhance local accountability. However, the proximity can breed rent-seeking behavior that is magnified as local governments are disinterested in collecting a visible tax on behalf of another level of government. Incentivizing the collectors with promise of higher pay is unlikely to solve the corruption problem.

Under modern functional arrangements, every attempt is made to minimize the distance between the tax administrator and the taxpayer, and this involves in particular to the collection function. In many cases, this involves payments in commercial banks or an increasing use of e-payments. There is a financial reconciliation function that typically also involves the Treasury.

Under modern systems, there needs to be a coordination of the treasury circuit and the tax administration. Payments could be made directly in banks, with a notification to the tax administration and the treasury. If the payments are subject to same day clearance with the Treasury Single Account (TSA) in the Government's account with the Central Bank, this could guide the setting of the payment limits for zero-balance accounts of local governments (if they have correspondent accounts in the TSA)—or direct payments within the specified spending limits notified and agreed with the local governments. Some large countries (Nigeria, China) may have state/provincial TSAs, but the same principles would apply to the respective sub-provincial governments. In all cases, it is important for the tax administration, treasury, and the municipal finance administrators to have at their disposal, full information of the funds being collected on their behalf and their ability to use these funds. This is a critical element of an improved governance framework, whether decentralized or other.

As we see in further detail below, to prevent corruption, the Senegalese system splits the assessment and the collection functions, assigned to the tax administration and the Treasury respectively. However, the process is cumbersome with poor exchange of information. It takes a long time, and many steps from the assessments made by the local tax offices to the handover of the total set of assessments by the Tax Administration in the Center to the Treasury, which then filters the demands back to the local officials (*receveurs*). These *receveurs* end up making their own assessments, ignoring the work done by the tax administration, and the objective of the administrative split breaks down. All the work is then performed by the local *receveurs*, defeating the objective of the split.

3.4 Enforcement

Typically, the enforcement function includes data management, including from third parties and open-source data (see below), and on the different stages of the collection process. The importance of keeping the data together cannot be overemphasized. This facilitates for example an exchange of information say between the VAT (that would typically also include new property transactions), the income taxes, and the property tax. One of the main weaknesses of the PIT in emerging market economies is that it is mainly a withholding tax on wages. Building up a picture on the ownership, use and transactions of physical assets, particularly property, is a critical element in expanding the base of the PIT. This can be achieved with the flow of information between different tax administrations (if they use a common Tax Identifier Number (TIN)) and agencies, or a central tax administration. It is a fundamental element in the determination of an audit plan (for all taxes). Indeed, the audit function is very difficult to decentralize, as both a warehouse of national information is needed, relative to the legal framework, as well as very specialized skills.

While countries are moving the property tax to the central administration, this may not work well unless the central tax authority itself is organized on a functional basis and the model being followed covers both the large taxpayers and a small taxpayer regime. If the structure of a tax administration only focuses on large taxpayers, e.g., through a Large Taxpayer

Unit (LTU), and the LTU absorbs most of the resources, the tax administration may have little incentive to operate a property tax (even if it improves the administration of the main taxes, such as the PIT). Thus, the integration of the property tax with the central administration requires an amendment in the structure and operation of the administration itself. This is nicely illustrated with the Tanzanian example.

3.5 Bill Delivery and Taxpayer Services

Under a self-assessment-based system it is the responsibility of the taxpayer to make the assessment and the payments. The onus is then on the tax administration to determine whether the process works as intended or whether an audit is needed. These functions could be handled by the local offices of the central tax administration or by local tax administrations.

4 New Technology: Blockchain Options

Blockchain options can revolutionize the flow of information on property registration and transactions, and simplify both the tax administration and treasury functions involved in local governance. The information is immutable and reduces possibilities of diversion of resources by "collectors" or different levels of government, enhancing the accountability for local administrations.

4.1 What Is Blockchain?

Blockchain refers to a family of technologies and organizational principles to create a "trustless public ledger"—an immutable public registry that is not under control of any single agent. This aspect of the blockchain makes it particularly appropriate for the decentralized management and storage of public data as a "commons." In particular, the "public ledger" aspect makes it a candidate for improving the management of data in the public sector, and, especially, for registering property ownership, rentals, and sales, as well as the treasury, and multilevel public financial management systems. Importantly, blockchain is being used increasingly for electronic property registration across the world.

Blockchain transactions are permanently recorded by appending blocks of information across many computers so that the record cannot be altered retroactively without the alteration of all subsequent blocks and the consensus of the network. It serves as a historical record of all transactions that ever occurred, from the genesis block to the latest block. Hence, the name blockchain.

A transaction is the transfer of a digital asset, or information between two parties. With cryptocurrencies, this digital asset is currency. However, it could also be a land deed (enabling ownership verification), or personal information (enabling digital identity control).

The revolutionary technology of the blockchain created the world's first genuine decentralized, peer-to-peer monetary system based on the use of Bitcoin, the first of many presently circulating types of cryptocurrencies.

4.2 *Digital Tools of Blockchain*

The two essential digital tools of the blockchain technology are hashes and smart contracts. A hash is a mathematical function that converts an input of arbitrary length into an encrypted output of a fixed length. Thus, regardless of the original amount of data, or file size involved, its unique hash will always have the same size. Moreover, hashes cannot "reverse-engineer" the input from the hashed output because hash functions work only uni-directionally.

Smart contracts are programs stored on a blockchain that run when predetermined conditions are met. They typically are used to automate the execution of an agreement so that all participants can be immediately certain of the outcome, without any intermediary's involvement, or time loss. For example, a user intending to insert a new transaction into the blockchain must follow specific rules for the operation. Missing them, for example, failing to specify the object of the transaction, will stop the process.

Every block contains information, through a hash, about a transaction (or a certain number of transactions). It also contains a reference, through another hash, to the preceding block in the blockchain, as well as an answer to a complex mathematical puzzle. This answer is used to validate the data associated with that block. A copy of the blockchain is stored on every computer in the network and these computers periodically synchronize to make sure that all of them have the same shared database. This provides for an exceptional degree of resiliency. Since the same copy of the blockchain is stored in multiple computers connected to the network, even if many computers fail at any given time, the shared database can be recreated in its entirety.

4.3 *Building a Blockchain*

Blockchain building and management consist of creating blocks, linking, and inserting them into the chain.

Blocks

The rectangles in Fig. 6.2 represent blocks. The first rectangle to the right contains a date; the hash, containing the encrypted identification of the previous block; a new hash, containing the information that will identify it, and information about a previous transaction. The block in the center has been accessed through the information provided by the previous block's hash. It has a new time-stamped and contains a new transaction. To be inserted in the blockchain, this block needs to be validated. This is done by mining. Mining a block refers to adding the block in the blockchain's network. A miner selects a set of transactions from the pool of transactions and then mines the block; or computes the hash to add the block to the network. If two or more miners mine the same block at the same time, the block with more difficulty is selected. The others are known as stale blocks. Mining usually rewards miners with blockchain currency, or when the blockchain is not used for creating a cryptocurrency with other means.

The process will continue with the creation, of a new block, such that at the left and its insertion in the blockchain.

Nodes

Blockchains consist of a network of computers, more exactly of nodes passing messages between each other. For example, every participant in a

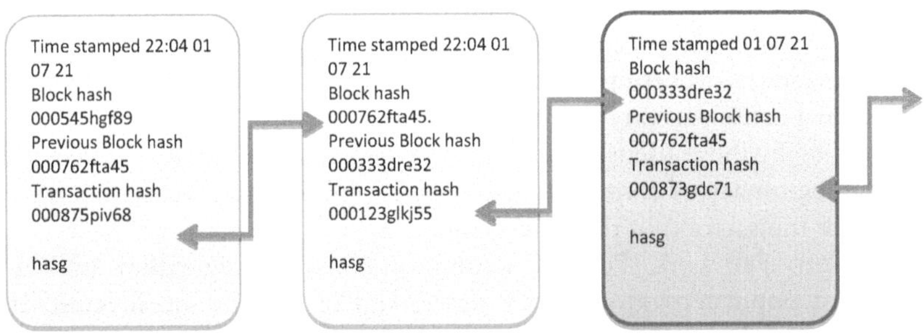

Fig. 6.2 Building blocks of blockchain

coin's network is a node. A node is a computer connected to the blockchain network. We have different types of nodes. Full nodes store a copy of the entire blockchain and thus guarantee the security and correctness of the data on the blockchain by validating data. Lightweight nodes contain only a partial list of a blockchain operation, which usually includes just the block headers, instead of its entire transaction history.

The node connected to the blockchain that helps in the execution of a transaction in return for an incentive is called miner. When a computer connects to the blockchain, a copy of the blockchain data gets downloaded into the system and the node comes in sync with the latest block of data on blockchain.

4.4 *Applying a Blockchain*

In any centralized system, like a database holding key information about, for example, driving licenses in a country, a central administrator has the authority to maintain and update the database. The task of making any updates—like adding/deleting/updating names of people who qualified for certain licenses—is performed by a central authority who remains the sole in-charge of maintaining genuine records. This arrangement is not very secure, and remains subject to abuse, giving rise to the need for reconciliation and audit—or a significant part of both tax and budget execution systems.

Public blockchains that operate as decentralized, self-regulating systems work on a global scale without any single authority. They involve contributions from hundreds of thousands of participants who work on verification and authentication of transactions occurring on the blockchain, and on the block mining activities. In such a dynamically changing status of the blockchain, these publicly shared ledgers need an efficient, fair, real-time, functional, reliable, and secure mechanism to ensure that all the transactions occurring on the network are genuine and all participants agree on a consensus on the status of the ledger. This all-important task is performed by the consensus mechanism, which is a set of rules that decides on the legitimacy of contributions made by the various participants (i.e., nodes or transactors) of the blockchain.

The proof of work (PoW) is a common consensus algorithm used by the most popular cryptocurrency networks like Bitcoin and litecoin. It requires a participant node to prove that the work done and submitted by them qualifies them to receive the right to add new transactions to the blockchain. However, the whole mining mechanism of Bitcoin needs a large amount of energy and a long processing time. The proof of stake (PoS) is another common consensus algorithm that evolved as a low-cost, low-energy consuming alternative to the PoW algorithm. It involves the allocation of responsibility in maintaining the public ledger to a participant node in proportion to the number of virtual currency tokens held by it.

4.5 Features and Strengths of Blockchain

The main features are as follows:

- *All data is notarized.* Blockchain data is immutable and time-stamped with a unique verification code (the hash). Thus, data cannot be changed. Amendments are marked with the time the change was made. This means that data cannot be tampered with. Corrupt officials cannot change the official records or make a property transaction disappear.
- *Accountability and access control.* Each time data is added a new block is added to the chain is both time-stamped and digitally signed by the person (or software) initiating the transaction. These signatures cannot be faked. This mechanism provides verified access control, limiting which data can be changed and by whom. The signature also provides mathematical proof of the origin of a transaction. This means in practical terms that all data in the database is marked with a mathematical proof of its origin. Together with the immutability and time-stamped properties, this effectively means that all data on the blockchain is notarized.
- *Data is distributed:* Blockchain also solves (or facilitates) the problem of public availability. The decentralized nature of the blockchain database means that there is no single point of failure. As we saw, each "full node" contains a complete copy of all the data that is constantly updated as new data is added, and as long as a single of such nodes exist, the service and the data will remain available. Blockchain technology, more precisely a consortium type of blockchain (see later for the illustration), is a suitable way of sharing—and editing—a database between different departments or branches of government—say between the Cadastral service and the Tax Administration, or between the latter and the Treasury.

- *Resilience:* A usual database architecture depends on a central server, a relatively fragile setup, subject to breaks or overloads, poor or interrupted internet access, and inadequate disaster relief and back-ups. These risks are mitigated using blockchain technology, as the database, and access to the data, is replicated in each "full node," which is regularly updated with the new blocks that are validated by the users. Anyone can set up and host such a full node. Municipalities could have their own copy of the blockchain for guaranteed and fast access, but so could, for example, do banks or other private companies. All these copies of the data add to the resilience of the system: they make it faster to access and less likely that data will be lost. This also means that information does not have to flow from banks to the Treasury Single Account and Central Tax Administration, and then return with lags to the local governments. Rather, the information is available immediately to all the relevant parties at different levels of government (and the public, in principle), greatly improving both the revenue and treasury circuits.
- *Access and safety*: "Write access" to the blockchain database is regulated by "public key technology," and rules for access are hardcoded in the software. This is a very potent system, in which access to data can be assigned in a very fine-grained way.
- *Security:* If a centralized database is hacked, data can be changed arbitrarily. The blockchain provides some additional safety against malicious actors. First, data cannot be changed retroactively (because of its "chained" structure and the fact there are many copies of the database, and unauthorized changes would be noticed immediately). Secondly, if a hacker steals the private key of any user, he can only have access to the data in as far as that user has that access. The data will only partly be compromised—and this can be identified and tracked to that user. Thus, the system can recover from such an attack, in particular, if the number of authorized users is known (as in a permissioned blockchain): access can be denied to the comprised key, and the hacked party can be assigned a new key.

  Further protection can be obtained by a "multisig"—requiring that certain transactions can be added to the blockchain only if they are signed off on by two or more parties. One can image, for example, that the transfer of property is only finalized when signed by the seller, the buyer, and the cadastral agency itself. Many scenarios can be envisaged.

- *Storing large amounts of data:* The fact that data is duplicated is one of the reasons that the blockchain is resilient. It also means that it is not the right medium to store large amounts of files. Photographs, scans of documents, and so on are not stored on the blockchain itself, but in a separate system. These documents can then be notarized on the blockchain via their "hash"—a number that uniquely identifies the document. This schema plays nicely with Inter Planetary File System (IPFS), in which files are stored under the same hash value, and has a duplication and replication schemes that are similar to those of the blockchain. A central agency—the cadaster itself—would then store all the original files, and any nodes would duplicate those files as needed to have them quickly locally available.

5 Types of Blockchain

After Satoshi Nakamoto (2008) introduced Bitcoin and Blockchain, other types of platforms have surfaced. We have basically three types:

1. Public (decentralized);
2. Private (centralized);
3. Consortium (a hybrid type that operates under the leadership of a group of member organizations, instead of a single entity).

The types are differentiated according to access, transaction making, viewing, and use, as illustrated in Table 6.1.

- The public/distributed version is the blockchain by antonomasia. There are no restrictions to access, transact, and view, provided rules and codes are observed. They can be set up by a group of individuals and modified according to the rules the group has established. Creation of cryptocurrencies is its main present use. However, many diversified uses are compatible.
- The private blockchain is set up by businesses and governments. The distinction between public and private is not related to the nature of ownership rights, but rather to excludability. Public blockchains are by design non-excludable, while private and consortium platforms are excludable. Property rights accruing to founders allow them to determine the rules governing access, transact, view, and, obviously,

Table 6.1 Types of blockchain

	Public/distributed	*Private*	*Consortium*
Access	No access restrictions	Invitation only by network administrators	Restricted to consortium members and to individuals and bodies designated by members
Transact	Anyone can transact	Only designated individuals	As for access
View	Anyone can view	Restricted. Only designated individuals. No public viewing	As for access and transact
Type and use	Large decentralized. Bitcoin, Ethereum, cryptocurrency.	Middle ground platforms: accounting record keeping procedures, cryptocurrencies	Participating members equally involved in the consensus and decision-making process

use. The latter includes record keeping, tracking of supply chains, airlines booking, and also cryptocurrencies.

- The consortium blockchain involves the participation of various organizations, both private and public that decide, among others, the degree of excludability from the platform.
- Hybrid blockchains (partially centralized and partially decentralized) have been developed starting from the three core types: needed balance between auditability, security, scalability, and data storage for applications build on top of them. The ability to control who has access for viewing and to regulate who is allowed to upload data without sacrificing autonomy and running the risk of exposing sensitive data to the public internet is a perfect example.

6 Blockchain and Land Surveying, Registration, and Taxation

Land governance, real estate management, urban planning, and property taxation rely on surveying and recording in registries, or cadasters. Surveying is an essential and crucial method of mapping land boundaries, distances, slopes, and features to legitimize parcel boundaries. It enables land development, from the planning and design of subdivisions to the final construction of roads, utilities, and landscaping. The same applies to buildings.

Satellite or aerial photography expands the frontiers of land and infrastructure surveying, technically and economically. In the urban areas zones are specified, and buildings in these zones are identified by drawing their outlines on the map. Each building is given a number and a code. Often, this is the first time these buildings are identified, and this method effectively gives them an address. This information is then entered in the database. The result is "Geodatabase" of properties. In addition to being a simple collection of data, it also comes with some data analysis functionality: the map can be rendered in different ways by coloring buildings based on use, value, tax liabilities, and so on.

Digital land registries/land registration is where documents, manifesting legal rights from a property transaction, are recorded. Matters concerning ownership, possession, or other rights of real property are recorded and preserved. Cadaster is the process of mapping those rights and subsequent storage of the mapping data. As we have illustrated, surveying, registration, and cadaster are the bedrock of property taxation. Blockchain technology facilitates these tasks and lowers their cost by offering the possibility of new institutional and organization forms, particularly with regard to taxation. Just to list a few examples:

- *Consortium blockchains allow* new business models known as Decentralized Autonomous Organizations. This could have implications for the design of tax administrations as well as budget and treasury systems, revolutionizing the flow of information across levels of government as well as with the public at large. A cadaster or register could be set up as a "permissioned blockchain": a small number of trusted parties are responsible for validating new blocks. These could be government agents or also private parties. The level of trust that needs to be placed on these validators is minimal—the possibility of changing and updating data is not under control of the validators. However, a certain amount of control over the blockchain remains in the hands of the validators. They can agree to "censor" certain operations; for example, if a private key is compromised, they can refuse to allow any updates signed by that key. Blockchain technology is a suitable way of sharing—and editing—a database between different departments or branches of government—say between the cadastral service and the tax administration, or between the latter and the treasury (see EU report by Ahmad, Brosio and Gerbrandy 2018, for use of blockchain for property tax administration).

- *Controlling access to write data:* This should be granted depending on the usage of the system, and the business model to be developed. A conservative classical solution could imagine that a central authority—the cadastral institute itself—assigns (and if necessary, retracts) the permissions to write data to specific areas to specific agents. For example, depending on organizational and legal context, it could assign the right to transfer property in municipality to that municipality only—or reserve the right for finalizing a transfer to a central authority. This system can arbitrarily be extended to include the taxpayers themselves, who may be, for example, given identifiable accounts into which taxes can be paid.
- *Private information on the blockchain:* The blockchain itself is public, but that does not mean that all data written on the blockchain is publicly available. While general cadastral data (where is the property, who owns it) is usually public, personal information that may be sensitive (did she pay her taxes on time) may not be. By encrypting such data, it is possible to save data on the blockchain that is readable only by selected parties,—for example, a payment may be visible only to (those who have access to the private key) of the payer and the tax authority.
- *Tokens with value:* One of the more interesting and potentially disruptive possibilities of the blockchain is to create "scarce digital objects": purely virtual objects that cannot be multiplied at zero marginal cost, as digital objects usually are. This means that one can create tokens that live on the blockchain and that have true value. This concept opens a large range of scenarios in which the payment themselves can be integrated in the system. In a classical approach, payments are handled by banks or other payment providers, and the tax authority must coordinate with each of these providers to match payments to taxpayer records in the registry. If payments can be made in the register itself makes this process more efficient.

  Under this scheme, the tax authority emits credits with a nominal value, as tokens on the blockchain. Taxpayers can now buy tax credits from the tax authority and pay their taxes directly on the blockchain—thereby reducing the procedure of payment and the processing of that payment in the tax administration to a single step, that is transparent to all parties involved. This schema is interesting

> not only because it simplifies the payment process for individual taxpayers and makes it less error prone. It also facilitates the creation of third-party services for payment of taxes. because it makes it possible for third parties to provide services to taxpayers in a "trustless way"—for example, a bank or a mobile payment provider such as M-Pesa or MaxLipo can integrate the possibility to pay taxes in their mobile applications without the need to coordinate with the tax authorities and without any financial risk for the tax authority or itself. Or the provider can buy tax credits from the authority and settle the tax payments for their clients directly on the blockchain.

Since 2016, Sweden's land registry authority, the Lantmäteriet, has been testing a way to record property transactions on a blockchain. This could save substantial amounts every year by eliminating paperwork, reducing fraud, and speeding up transactions. Whereas the first phase was essentially a presentation of the technology's potential, the latest phase involved the creation of smart contracts that automate transactions on a blockchain. For instance, instead of the buyer and seller signing a bill of sale at the agent's office, this can now be done with digital signatures that are verified automatically.

Blockchain technology could in principle allow countries to "leapfrog" institutional and technology constraints. The possibilities are quite exciting and could be developed further with experimentation. Ironically, in countries with weak institutions and procedures, the blockchain options may be easier to introduce, as there is less that needs to be dismantled, and what is there does not work very well in any case.

References

Ahmad E., (2015) Governance and Institutions. In Ahmad E, and Brosio, G., (eds) Handbook of Multilevel Finance. Edward Elgar, Cheltenham

Ahmad E, N Stern, (1991) The theory and practice of tax reform in developing countries. Cambridge University Press.

Ahmad E, G Brosio and C Pöschl, (2015) Local property taxes and benefits in developing countries: overcoming political resistance? In: Ahmad E, and Brosio G (eds) Handbook of Multilevel Finance. Edward Elgar, Cheltenham

Ahmad E, Brosio G and Gerbrandy J., (2018) Property taxation Economic features, revenue potential and administrative issues in a development context. EU, Brussels.

Bird R., (2011) Subnational Taxation in Developing Countries: A Review of the Literature, Journal of International Commerce, Economics and Policy, 2(1), 139-161.

Blažić H, Stašić S, Drezgić S., (2014) The Administrative Costs of Local Government Property-Based User Charges and Their Regressivity. International Public Administration Review 9 (4) 7-29.

De Cesare C., (2016) Relevancia del impuesto inmobiliario. In De Cesare C (ed) Sistemas del Impuesto Predial en América Latina y el Caribe. Lincoln Institute, Cambridge Mass.

Kalkuhl M, Fernandez Milan B, Schwerhoff G, Jakob M, Hahnen M and Creutzig F., (2017) Fiscal Instruments for Sustainable Development: The Case of Land Taxes, Mercator Research Institute on Global Commons and Climate Change.

Satoshi N., (2008) Bitcoin: a Peer-to-peer electronic cash system.

CHAPTER 7

Toward a Beneficial Property Tax Agenda for Sustainable Growth

Abstract In this chapter we link the need for a more effective local own-source revenue base to the sustainable growth agenda. The argument for a beneficial property tax on non-business properties, based on simple criteria, is highlighted, given the need to generate revenues quickly, and in an equitable manner. The tax-benefit link is critical for political economy purposes under all economic systems, as well as the simplification using area/location and occupancy. A functional administration permits arm's length operations, along with satellite imagery and blockchain technology. A strengthened property tax would reduce the need for reliance on land sales, which has huge environmental and adverse distributional consequences. However, it should be part of a broader reform that also includes within province/state fiscal equalization to avoid generating unsustainable migration incentives to mega metropolises, some of which are sinking, like Mexico City and Jakarta.

Keywords Taxation of property • Tax reform • Sustainable urban growth • Local accountability • Tax-benefits links

Societies and governments all over the world are facing huge common challenges to shield the planet from climate warming disasters to the ways of preparing societies to confront the likely occurrence of new pandemics,

E. Ahmad, G. Brosio, *Beneficial Property Taxation for Emerging Market Countries*, https://doi.org/10.1007/978-3-031-08612-0_7

whose frequency is likely to increase in an ever more physically interrelated world. Societies are witnessing, and suffering from, the increased emergence of global public bads. They require an increasingly urgent response in the quantity of public global goods and services, most of which are locally provided. Local governments are at the frontline of the costly responses and need additional resources. Moreover, in a context of growing wealth inequality, the weakest level determines the effectiveness of the responses. The strength of a chain is equal to the strength of the weakest link, requiring support from the richest individuals, or governments to the poorest ones.

Much of the additional financing needs will arise from transfers from higher levels of international community. But for effective use of these funds, tighter monitoring is needed, along with own-source revenues at the margin. The own-source revenues also open sustainable access to private finance. Yet, poorly designed transfers and absence of effective own-source revenues can lead to irresponsible local behavior and do more harm than good. We draw lessons for policy makers in this chapter, drawing on the new developments in method, information generation and management, and recent country experiences.

The premise on which this volume is based is that local governments are the front players in addressing adaptation challenges for sustainable employment growth. The local tier will need considerable strengthening, including additional financial resources that should be disbursed and managed in a responsible manner. Own source revenues are critical in ensuring local accountability, and ensuring access to private finance in a responsible manner, and the main lever is the property tax. It has significant revenue potential in relation to local spending, as well as important efficiency features. However, these potentialities are seldom exploited. Collections in most emerging market countries are, with rare exceptions, dismal.

The causes of the failure of the value-based property tax, and by extension, land-value capture that depends on accurately measuring changes in value with betterment levies, lie in design that is often inappropriate in most emerging market countries (also noticed by Margaret Thatcher in the UK), and the complexity of administration that opens the doors to rent-seeking in many cases. In principle the idea that people should be taxed on changes in their asset values (including the basis for land value capture financed investments) appears efficient and rational, but requires real-time monitoring of asset price changes, including for land and built-up properties, and reflecting these in a timely manner into the cadasters for tax purposes. This is the practice in advanced countries like the US for all properties, and for business properties in most countries, as an active market exists, including in the UK and China. Thus, the biggest infrastructure project in Europe, London's Crossrail, is partially funded by a betterment levy on business, but not households, and also relies on guaranteed loans and grants from the central government.

The value-based system is problematic as a recurrent tax for non-business (household) properties and has led to disappointing outcomes in most emerging market economies. The value-based model is built on two components. First, the tax base is defined as the money value of properties. The task of the administration is, then to approximate, as accurately as possible, prevailing market price and its variations. Second, cadastral methods, including their modern variants, are the key instruments for the assessment of the tax base. In reality, cadasters are costly and cumbersome, requiring the compilation of large amounts of legal and economic information, and are prone to large delays in updating information. This produces large gaps between market values and assessed values that is, in turn, the source of conflicts between the fisc and the taxpayers. These problems are obviously more acute in emerging market and lower-income countries, because of costs and capacity constraints.

We have proposed in this volume, a radically simpler alternative consisting in the adoption of the area-based model, where the tax base is defined according to the size and the location of properties and, where appropriate, also with use of a very few verifiable variables, such as use, age, or type of properties. The area/location basis for the property tax provides a reasonable approximation of market values with much lighter administration requirements. Simpler registers replace cadasters, relevant information is frequently available and/or can be provided by the taxpayers.

It is possible to sidestep the legal issues involved in establishing ownership by changing the base to occupancy. This has the advantage of being relatively simple and quick to administer, especially in countries with unclear or communal property titles. And an important advantage is that it also provides a recognition of residency for the informal sector households to be able to qualify for access to public services and bank loans. The alternative for informal sector households is either no access to public health or basic education or often expensive private alternatives.

Simplicity of methods does not exclude but is rather tied to the use of digital technologies, such digital imagery, and of distributed public ledgers like the blockchain, as illustrated at length in the volume. An added advantage of blockchain is that verified information is available to the tax authorities, municipalities, and the central government at the same time—so the costly and ineffective trickle down of revenue numbers is avoided. Consequently, transparency and simplicity in the public financial management arrangements becomes a distinct possibility. This could help avoid the problems seen in Senegal where the local authorities have no idea of what has been collected in property tax and what might eventually trickle down to their bank accounts. In the absence of clear revenue flows and assured revenue shares and transfers together with a lack of clarity in what the functions of the local government are, and on control over key economic elements like control over hiring decisions or the wage and investment decisions, the local budget becomes an exercise in futility.

The political economy considerations of the property tax are extremely important. Taxpayers' hostility to the tax would be attenuated by the establishment of direct linkages between the burden of the tax and the benefits received, for example, local public services including basic education and health care, provided by local governments. This linkage created the conditions for the property tax to qualify for Alfred Marshall's beneficial tax. Linkages can be strengthened by the use of location of properties, as a main determinant of the property tax. They can be further fostered by illustrating how total collections will be divided between areas of expenditure. This amounts to specifying the rates according to costs of service delivery, as in the UK. Thus, the tax rates would vary by adjustments in cost structure that are much more stable than property market prices.

The focus on land value capture to finance local infrastructure, including investments needed for adaptation of cities climate change considerations, needs to be more carefully tempered to the specific context. There are two elements involved—capturing the increase in values through betterment taxes or levies, or land sales to private developers who then undertake to provide the infrastructure through various combinations of PPPs. The first component can only function if all properties are subject to a value-based property tax that reflects market prices instantaneously, as in the US or Japan. In the UK this applies only to business properties. Betterment levies only on businesses remain a possibility for emerging market countries, and in transition countries like China, although there may be concerns about adding to the cost of doing business that might negate the objectives of the investments.

Land sales were successful in China in providing local finances as tax bases were centralized and a recurrent tax on non-business properties did not exist, other than in the pilot cities Shanghai and Chongqing but which had failed to raise revenues. Wang et al. (2018) pointed to the resulting tendency of urban sprawl, loss of prime agricultural land and wetlands, rent-seeking behavior by the developers and local governments, as well as increasing spatial and interpersonal inequalities. Another huge problem was the magnitude of off-budget liabilities that were being generated, with developers like Evergrande operating effective Ponzi schemes that became apparent as the authorities imposed prudential guidelines.

This volume has made use of various arguments derived from the theory and the observation of practice, where the competing models work or do not as in the value-based model in Senegal and Tanzania. We have also presented the results of the simulation of the implementation of the area-based property tax in two large emerging countries, China and Mexico, showing that revenues closer to potential can be raised quickly, and the process is inequality reducing especially in the case of a direct linkage with basic services.

China has no recurrent property tax on households at present and is beginning new pilots to replace the land sales model. The Mexican property tax is dysfunctional and the bulk of the country's property tax revenues are generated in Mexico City and a few other major metro areas that end up generating huge service delivery disparities that again influence migrants from lagging regions. The results of the simulations are very encouraging in terms of revenue and also of equity, especially when the equity impact of the introduction of the tax is estimated within a balanced budget framework (Musgrave 1959). In this framework the impact of the tax on distribution of income is compared to the impact on the income distribution deriving from the expenditure the tax is financing. In both cases the balanced budget impact is positive improving the distribution and with reference to different types of expenditure, going from the social to the education sectors. Very interestingly, in the case of Mexico, a new area-based tax would fare better in terms of equity than the present dysfunctional value-based model even without the benefit linkages. However, the benefit linkages are to be recommended for political economy and accountability objectives.

We have also directed attention to the trait of the property tax as an autonomous source of revenue for local governments implying a discretionary although limited, power of determining the tax rate according to the financial needs.

Finally, an enhanced use of the property tax will favor disproportionally the richer jurisdictions, and this will enhance spatial inequalities in service delivery. This will prevent the development of clean compact cities as new "employment hubs" to reduce pressures on polluted and overcrowded metro areas, such as Mexico City or Jakarta that are actually sinking. Poor jurisdictions need support for equity and efficiency purposes. Equalization grants are the interface of the property tax and of an inclusive, sustainable, and resilient growth strategy.

References

Musgrave R. (1959) The theory of public finance: a study in public economy. McGraw-Hill, New York

Wang W, Wu A and Ye F I (2018) "Land use reforms: towards sustainable development in China," in Ahmad, Niu and Xiao (eds) op cit.

Annex Table 1 Detailed structure of property taxation in selected countries

	1990	*2000*	*2010*	*2018*	*2019*
Chile. Taxes on property, total	**1.0**	**1.3**	**0.8**	**1.1**	**1.1**
Recurrent taxes on immovable property	0.6	0.7	0.6	0.7	0.8
Recurrent taxes on net wealth	0.0	0.0	0.0	0.0	0.0
Estate, inheritance, and gift taxes	0.0	0.0	0.0	0.1	0.0
Taxes on financial and capital transactions	0.4	0.6	0.2	0.3	0.3
Colombia. Taxes on property, total	**0.2**	**1.0**	**1.6**	**1.5**	**1.8**
Recurrent taxes on immovable property	0.2	0.5	0.6	0.8	0.8
Recurrent taxes on net wealth	0.0	0.0	0.4	0.0	0.1
Estate, inheritance, and gift taxes	0.0	0.0	0.0	0.0	0.0
Taxes on financial and capital transactions	0.0	0.5	0.6	0.7	0.8
France. Taxes on property, total	**2.6**	**3.0**	**3.5**	**4.0**	**3.9**
Recurrent taxes on immovable property	1.4	1.8	2.4	2.5	2.4
Recurrent taxes on net wealth	0.2	0.2	0.2	0.1	0.1
Estate, inheritance, and gift taxes	0.4	0.5	0.4	0.6	0.6
Taxes on financial and capital transactions	0.6	0.5	0.5	0.8	0.8
Israel. Taxes on property, total	**..**	**3.1**	**3.3**	**3.2**	**3.1**
Recurrent taxes on immovable property	..	2.1	2.1	1.9	1.9
Recurrent taxes on net wealth	..	0.0	0.0	0.0	0.0
Estate, inheritance, and gift taxes	..	0.0	0.0	0.0	0.0
Taxes on financial and capital transactions	..	0.6	0.5	0.5	0.5
Non-recurrent taxes	..	0.5	0.7	0.7	0.7
Mexico. Taxes on property, total	**0.2**	**0.2**	**0.3**	**0.3**	**0.3**
Recurrent taxes on immovable property	0.1	0.1	0.2	0.2	0.2
Recurrent taxes on net wealth	0.0	0.0	0.0	0.0	0.0

E. Ahmad, G. Brosio, *Beneficial Property Taxation for Emerging Market Countries*, https://doi.org/10.1007/978-3-031-08612-0

	1990	*2000*	*2010*	*2018*	*2019*
Estate, inheritance, and gift taxes	0.0	0.0	0.0	0.0	0.0
Taxes on financial and capital transactions	0.1	0.1	0.1	0.1	0.1
Turkey. Taxes on property, total	**0.3**	**0.7**	**1.0**	**1.0**	**1.0**
Recurrent taxes on immovable property	0.0	0.1	0.2	0.2	0.2
Recurrent taxes on net wealth	0.0	0.0	0.0	0.0	0.0
Estate, inheritance, and gift taxes	0.0	0.0	0.0	0.0	0.0
Taxes on financial and capital transactions	0.3	0.6	0.8	0.8	0.7
China. Taxes on property			1.3	1.4	1.4
Recurrent taxes on immovable property			0.5	0.6	0.5
Household recurrent taxes on immovable property			0.0	0.0	0.0
Business recurrent taxes on immovable property			0.5	0.6	0.5
House property tax			0.2	0.3	0.3
Urban and town land use tax			0.2	0.3	0.2
Recurrent taxes on net wealth			0.0	0.0	0.0
Estate, inheritance, and gift taxes			0.0	0.0	0.0
Taxes on financial and capital transactions			0.9	0.9	0.9
Stamp tax on securities transactions			0.1	0.1	0.1
Other stamp duties			0.1	0.1	0.1
Deed tax			0.6	0.6	0.6

Sources: OECD revenue statistics 2021

https://www.oecd-ilibrary.org/sites/6e87f932-en/1/4/1/index.html?itemId=/content/publication/6e87f932-en&_csp_=989e3029323a6936ab9fa6df32f709e4&itemIGO=oecd&itemContentType=book#section-d1e710389

Source: https://stats.oecd.org/index.aspx?DataSetCode=RS_ASI

References

Ahmad E., (2015) Governance and Institutions. In Ahmad E, and Brosio, G., (eds) Handbook of Multilevel Finance. Edward Elgar, Cheltenham

Ahmad E., (2017) Political economy of tax reforms for the SDGs—improving the investment climate, addressing inequality, and stopping the cheating, Background Paper for the G24 Countries.

Ahmad, E., (2018) "Rebalancing in China—Fiscal Policies for sustainable Growth," Singapore Economic Review, 2018, 63(4), 861-884.

Ahmad, E., (2021) "National and Subnational Tax Reforms to Address Informality," in C. Deléchat and L. Medina, eds., The Global Informal Workforce, IMF, Washington DC, 2021.

Ahmad, E., (2021), "Multilevel financing of sustainable infrastructure in China—Policy options for inclusive, resilient and green growth". Journal of Infrastructure, Policy and Development, April.

Ahmad E, and R Searle, (2006) On the implementation of transfers to subnational governments. In: Ahmad and Brosio (eds) Handbook of Fiscal Federalism, Edward Elgar, Cheltenham

Ahmad E, N Stern, (1991) The theory and practice of tax reform in developing countries. Cambridge University Press.

Ahmad E, and Viscarra H., (2020a) Financing Clean, Compact and Connected Cities in Mexico: role of a "beneficial" property tax, LSE Program on Sustainable Transitions in China and Mexico.

Ahmad, E., and Viscarra H., (2020b) Fiscal Equalization for Basic Services and Preventive Health Care - Reforming Participaciones in Mexico, LSE Program on SustainableTransitions in China and Mexico.

E. Ahmad, G. Brosio, *Beneficial Property Taxation for Emerging Market Countries*, https://doi.org/10.1007/978-3-031-08612-0

Ahmad, E., G. Brosio, P. Spahn and C. Vehorn (1995) Colombia: Reforming Territorial Taxation and Transfers, IMF Fiscal Affairs Department, Washington DC.

Ahmad E, K. Li, T. Richardson, (2002) Recentralization in China? In: Ahmad Tanzi (ed) Managing Fiscal Decentralization, Routledge

Ahmad E, Gonzalez Anaya J, Brosio G, García-Escribano M, Lockwood B, and Revilla E., (2007) Why Focus on Spending Needs Factors? The Political Economy of Fiscal Transfer Reforms in Mexico. Imf Working Papers.

Ahmad E, Rydge J, and Stern N., (2013) Structural change drives tax reforms drives structural change, LSE, presented at the China Development Forum.

Ahmad E, G Brosio and C Pöschl, (2015) Local property taxes and benefits in developing countries: overcoming political resistance? In: Ahmad E, and Brosio G (eds) Handbook of Multilevel Finance. Edward Elgar, Cheltenham

Ahmad E, Brosio G and Gerbrandy J., (2018a) Property taxation Economic features, revenue potential and administrative issues in a development context. EU, Brussels.

Ahmad, E., Niu M, and Xiao K., (2018b) Fiscal Policies for Sustainable Development in China—Rebalancing in Guangdong. Springer.

Ahmad, E., D. Dowling, D. Chan, S. Colenbrander and N. Godfrey, (2019), Scaling up investment for sustainable urban infrastructure: A guide to national and subnational reform, Coalition for Urban Transitions: A New Climate Economy Initiative.

Ahmad, E, Niu M, and Wang L., (2020) Designing Beneficial Property Taxation for Sustainable Development in China-evidence from six cities, including Guangzhou. LSE/CUT Program on Financing Sustainable Urban Transitions in China and Mexico.

Ahmad, E., Meili Niu, Liming Wang, Meiyan Wang, 2021. "Designing Beneficial Property Taxation for Sustainable Development in China—evidence from six cities, including Guangzhou" LSE Program on Financing Sustainable Urban Transitions in China and Mexico.

Anglin, Paul M., David Dale-Johnson, Yanmin Gao, and Guozhong Zhu, (2014) "Patterns of Growth in Chinese Cities: Implications of the Land Lease," Journal of Urban Economics, 2014, 83 (C), 87–107.

Awasthi R, and Nagarajan M., (2020) Property Taxation in India: Issues Impacting Revenue Performance and Suggestions for Reform. The World Bank. Washington DC

Bahl, R., (2011), "Intergovernmental fiscal relations in local public finance," in Man, Joyce and Y-H Hong, (2011), China's Local Public Finance in Transition, Cambridge, Massachusetts: Lincoln Institute of Land Policy.

Bahl R., Wallace S (2008) Reforming the Property Tax in Developing countries. A new approach. Working Paper 08-19. Andrew School of Policy Studies.

Banobras (1997) La ModernizacionCatastral en elPrograma de 100 Ciudades. RevistaFederalismo y Desarrollo. No. 58

Banobras (2012), Excel Data Sheet, *Banco Nacional de Obras y Servicios Publicos.*

Bird R., (1999) Threading the Fiscal Labyrinth: Some Issues in Fiscal Decentralization. In Slemdod, Joel (ed) Tax Policy in the Real World. Cambridge University Press, New York.

Bird R., (2011) Subnational Taxation in Developing Countries: A Review of the Literature, Journal of International Commerce, Economics and Policy, 2(1), 139-161.

Bird R, and Rao, G., (2012) Coping with Change: The Need to Restructure Urban Governance and Finance in India. Institute on Municipal Finance and Governance.

Bird R. and Slack E., (2002) Land and Property Taxation: A Review. The World Bank

Bird R. and Slack E., (2014) Local Taxes And Local Expenditures In Developing Countries: Strengthening The Wicksellian Connection. Public Administration and Development. (wileyonlinelibrary.com.DOI: 10.1002/pad.1695

Blažić H, Stašić S, Drezgić S., (2014) The Administrative Costs of Local Government Property-Based User Charges and Their Regressivity. International Public Administration Review 9 (4) 7-29.

Brys, Bert, Stephen Matthews, Richard Herd, and Xiao Wang, (2013), "Tax Policy and Tax Reform in the Peoples Republic of China," **OECD Taxation Working Papers**, No. 18, OECD Publishing, Paris.

Buterin V., (2014) A Next-Generation Smart Contract and Decentralized Application Platform

Cabrero Mendoza E., (1995) La NuevaGestiónMunicipal en México. Análisis de ExperienciasInnovadoras en Gobiernos Locales. CIDE Mexico City.

Cabrero Mendoza E., and Nava Campos G., (1999) GerenciaPúblicaMunicipal: Conceptos Básicos y Estudios de Caso. CIDE, Mexico City.

Cabrero Mendoza, Enrique (2006) "Los Retos Institucionales de la descentral-izacion fiscal en America Latina", CIDE, division de Administración Pública Documento de Trabajo, No 181.

Cao, Jing and Wenhao Hu, (2016), "A Microsimulation of Property Tax Policy in China," Journal of Housing Economics.

Choi, Ki-Whan and David L. Sjoquist, (2014), "Economic and Spatial Effects of Land Value Taxation in an Urban Area: An Urban Computable General Equilibrium Approach," Land Economics, 91, 536–555.

Collier P, and Jones P., (2016) Transforming Dar es Salaam into a City that Works, https://urbanisation.econ.ox.ac.uk/materials/papers/73/collierjonesdaressalaam.p

Collier P, Glaeser E, Venables T., Manwaring P and Blake M (2018) Land and property taxes for municipal finance. International Growth Center, Oxford.

Dale-Johnson, David, Guozhong Zhu (2017), "Transition to the Property Tax in China: A Dynamic General Equilibrium Analysis", Working Paper WP17DD1, Lincoln Institute of Land Policy.

De Cesare C., (2016) Relevancia del impuesto inmobiliario. In De Cesare C (ed) Sistemas del Impuesto Predial en América Latina y el Caribe. Lincoln Institute, Cambridge Mass.

Development Research Center (DRC) of the State Council and the World Bank, 2014, Urban China: toward efficient, inclusive and sustainable urbanization, World Bank, Washington DC.

Ding, Chengri, (2005) "Property Tax Development in China," Land Lines, 17:3.

Fjeldstad O-H, and Katera L., (2017) Taxing the urban boom in Tanzania: central-local government relations in property tax collection in Tanzania REPOA's 22nd Annual Research Workshop.

Foster C, Jackman D R, and Perlman M., (1980) Local Government Finance in a Unitary State, George Allen and Unwin, Hemel Hempstead.

Franzsen R, William McCluske (eds) (2017) Property Tax In Africa Status, Challenges, and Prospects. Lincoln Center for Land Policy. Cambridge Mass.

Grover R, Walacik M, Buzu O, Gunes T, Raskovic M, Yildiz M., (2019) Barriers to the use of property taxation in municipal finance, Journal of Financial Management of Property and Construction 24(02), 166–83.

Hausman R. et al. (2016) Atlas of Economic Complexity, Harvard-MIT Complexity Project.

IMF (2017) Senegal: Staff Report for the 2016 Consultation, CR 17/02, p. 36.

INDETEC (2013) Revista Hacienda Municipal.

Kalantari, M, and La, V (2015) Assessing OpenStreetMap as an Open Property MapI in: OpenStreetMap in GIScience 2015: 255-272.

Kalkuhl M, and Edenhofer M., (2016) Ramsey Meets Thünen: The Impact of Land Taxes on Economic Development and Land Conservation. International Tax and Public Finance, 1–31. 24 (2): 350-380

Kalkuhl M, Fernandez Milan B, Schwerhoff G, Jakob M, Hahnen M and Creutzig F., (2017) Fiscal Instruments for Sustainable Development: The Case of Land Taxes, Mercator Research Institute on Global Commons and Climate Change.

Khan Q, Khawja A, and Olken B., (2016) Tax farming redux, experimental evidence on performance pay for tax collectors', Quarterly Journal of Economics. 131 (1): 219-271.

Kireyev A, and Mansur A., (2015) Making Senegal a Hub for West Africa, IMF.

Kumar D, and Raychaudhuri T., (1982) The Cambridge Economic History of India: Vol.1. Cambridge University Press.

Lindahl E., (1919) Just taxation – A positive solution. In Classics in Musgrave R, Peacock A (eds) The Theory of Public Finance. Macmillan: London, 1964; 85–98.

Liu, He, (2018a) 3 critical battles China is preparing to fight. Speech to World Economic Forum, Davos, January 24, 2018.

Zhi Liu (2018b) Land-Based Finance and Property Tax in China, ATI Working Paper.

Local Government Authority, Tanzania (2014). Fiscal inequities and the challenges of 'disadvantaged' LGAs.

Lou Jiwei (1997), "Constraints in reforming the Transfer System in China," in Ahmad, E., ed., Financing Decentralized Expenditures: An international comparison of grants," Edward Elgar, 1997.

Luo X, and Zhu N., (2020) Migration, City attractiveness and Regional Hubs in China, LSE/CUT Program on Financing Sustainable Urban Transitions in China and Mexico.

Man, Joyce, (2011), "Local Public Finance in China: An Overview," in Joyce Yanyun Man and Yu-Hung Hong, eds., 2011, China's Local Public Finance in Transition, Cambridge, Massachusetts: Lincoln Institute of Land Policy.

Marshall A., (1890) Principles of Economics (8th ed.), Macmillan & Co. Appendix G. Edition used: Principles of Economics. Macmillan and Co., London (8th ed. 1920), Online Library of Liberty.

McCluskey W J, Plimmer F, Connelan O., (1998) Ad valorem property tax. Issues of fairness an Equity Assessment Journal. 5 47-55.

Mieszkowski P., (1972) The property tax: An excise tax or a profits tax? Journal of Public Economics. 1 (1): 73-9.

Mirrlees Report (2011) Tax by design, Chapter 16. The Taxation of Land and Property. Institute for Fiscal Studies.

Morones Hernandez, H., (2011) Aumentar la RecaudacionPredial: Reto de la Hacienda Municipal: Por quélasreformas y políticas han tenido poco impacto en la recaudación. Revista Hacienda Municipal. 114: 112-124

Morones Hernandez, Humberto (2011) "Aumentar la Recaudacion Predial: reto de la Hacienda Municipal" Revista Hacienda Municipal, July-Sept, 2011: p.121.

Morones Hernandez, Humberto (2012), "Por que los Avances en la Modernizacion Catastral no se han Traducido en una Exitosa Recaudacion Predial". July-Sept 2012.

Muller A. (2000) Property Taxes And Valuation In Denmark, Presented at an OECD Seminar about Property Tax Reforms and Valuation. Vienna.

Musgrave R. (1959) The theory of public finance: a study in public economy. McGraw-Hill, New York

Norregaard J., (2013) Taxing Immovable Property Revenue Potential and Implementation Challenges. IMF Working Paper

Oates W., (1972) Fiscal Federalism. Harcourt Brace Jovanovich, New York

OECD (2021) A Review of Local Government Finance in Israel: Reforming the Arnona System, OECD Multi-level Governance Studies, OECD Publishing, Paris, https://doi.org/10.1787/a5bc4d25-en.

Olima W., (2010) Property Taxation in Anglophone East Africa: Case Study of Mauritius 2010 Lincoln Institute of Land Policy.

Palameta B, and Macredie I., (2005) Property taxes relative to income. Statistics Canada, Perspectives, March.

Peña Ahumada, J A, and WencePartida, L A., (2011) La Distribución de Transferencias Federales para Municipios. Revista Hacienda Municipal.115: 79-96

Peña Ahumada and Wence Partida, (2011). "La Distribución de Transferencias Federales para Municipios", Revista Hacienda Municipal, Oct-Dec.: p.90.

Piketty T, Yang L, and Zucman G., (2017) Capital Accumulation, Private Property and Rising Inequality in China, 1978-2015, WID.world Working Paper Series N° 2017/6

Raich Portman, Uri (2004) "Impacto de la descentralización del gasto en los municipios mexicanos", CIDE, Division de Economia, Documento de trabajo No.281.

Salm, M., (2017), Property tax in BRICS megacities, Springer.

Satoshi N., (2008) Bitcoin: a Peer-to-peer electronic cash system.

Shkabatur J, Saki K. (2014) Interactive community mapping: improving service delivery and empowering communities. http://documents.worldbank.org/curated/en/191751468326366823/pdf/890870WP0Box380munity0Mapping0final.pdf

Stuart Mill, J., (1848) Principles of Political Economy with some of their Applications to Social Philosophy. Book V, Chapter V Of Some Other Taxes, First Pub. Longmans, Green and Co.London

Stuart A, Emmerson C and Kenley A., (2007) A Survey of UK Local Government Finance, Institute for Fiscal Studies, London

Tiebout C., (1956). A Pure Theory of Local Expenditures, Journal of Political Economy, University of Chicago Press, vol. 64, pages 416.

UK Government Chief Scientific Adviser (2016) Distributed Ledger Technology: beyond block chain A report. http://www.ameda.org.eg/files/gs-16-1-distributed-ledger-technology.pdf

Vickrey W., (1963) General and specific financing of urban services. In Public Expenditure Decisions in the Urban Community. In Schaller H (ed) Resources for the Future: Washington; 62–90.

Wang W, Wu A and Ye F I (2018) "Land use reforms: towards sustainable development in China," in Ahmad, Niu and Xiao (eds) op cit.

Weingast B., (2009) Second Generation of Fiscal Federalism: The implications of fiscal incentives". Journal of Urban Economics. 65, (3) :279-293.

WEF (World Economic Forum). (2018), The Inclusive Growth and Development Report.

Wenban Smith H B., (2014) Population growth, internal migration and urbanization in Tanzania, 1967-2012. A Census based regional analysis. International Growth Center, Working Paper.

Wicksell K, (1896) A new principle of just taxation. In Classics in the Theory of Public Finance, Musgrave R, Peacock A (eds). Macmillan: London, 1964; 72–118.
Wildasin D (1987) Theoretical analysis of local public economics, S. Millls (ed.), Handbook of Regional and Urban Economics, Elsevier,
Wildasin D, and Wilson J D, (1991) Theoretical issues in local public economics. An overview, Regional Science and Urban Economics.
World Bank (2002) Dar Es Salaam Case Study Overview Climate Change, Disaster Risk And The Urban Poor: Cities Building Resilience For A Changing World,
Wright A, P De Filippi (2017) Decentralized blockchain technology and the rise of Lex Cryptographia. Available at https://perma.ccK/7HM-4GG7.
Xiao K., (2018) Managing subnational liability for sustainable development: a case study of Guangdong, in Ahmad, Niu and Xiao (2018), op cit.
Youngman J, Malme J., (2004) The property tax in a new environment: Lessons from international Tyax reform effort, Lincoln land institute. Cambridge Mass.
Zhi Liu (2018) Land-Based Finance and Property Tax in China, ATI Working Paper.
Zodrow G., (2006) Who Pays the Property Tax? Land Lines. 18, (2): 14-19.
Zodrow G, and Mieszkowski P., (1986) Pigou, Tiebout, Property Taxation and the Underprovision of Local Public Goods. Journal of Urban Economics 19, 356-370.

Index[1]

[1] Note: Page numbers followed by 'n' refer to notes.

E. Ahmad, G. Brosio, *Beneficial Property Taxation for Emerging Market Countries*, https://doi.org/10.1007/978-3-031-08612-0

The manufacturer's authorised representative in the EU is Springer Nature Customer Service Centre GmbH, Europaplatz 3, 69115 Heidelberg, Germany. If you have any concerns regarding our products, please contact ProductSafety@springernature.com

Printed and bound by CPI Group (UK) Ltd, Croydon, CR0 4YY

22/09/2026

02220948-0011